Cities of the World:

VIENNA

Cities of the World:

VIENNA

CHRISTA ESTERHÁZY

with 25 photographs and 2 maps

South Brunswick
New York: A. S. Barnes and Co.

A. S. Barnes and Co., Inc.
Cranbury, New Jersey 08512

6624

Printed in the United States of America

Contents

List of Illustrations

TO PALI

Chapter 1

Myth and Reality

THERE are innumerable myths about Vienna. There's the one about romantic Vienna, another about gay Vienna, a third about tragic Vienna. What is myth and what reality? Because of the many different characters given to their city by others, the Viennese themselves sometimes wonder. The facts can, of course, be found in any good guide-book, 'Go down the Graben, turn left and you will see one of the most imposing Gothic works of art, St Stephen's Cathedral . . .' and it is true that there are art and history around every corner in Vienna. But what of life today in this city of nearly a million and three-quarter people, a city consisting of twenty-four *Bezirke* or districts, only one-third of which can be called fully built-up areas? There is a breath of country air, even in the midst of brick and mortar.

It is a prosperous city and a hard-working one. Nearly everyone who wants it can have a job, and factories start at 7 a.m., while private and public offices open their doors at 8 a.m. Before the sunrise the sound of horses' hoofs, of heavy carts and the clatter of milk cans being unloaded make many a Viennese stir in his sleep. By 6.30 a.m. dairies and bakers are open and there are crisp *Semmeln* and *Kipferln* on the breakfast tables together with steaming cups of milk coffee.

Trams clank by; the Stadtbahn, a sort of primitive underground and overhead railway combined, which at times suggests a scenic railway, rattles over innumerable bridges, and suburban diesel trains on the newly developed Schnellbahn cross Vienna at considerable speed. The Viennese are very conservative and they hate moving house. They may have a job at one end of the town and live right at the other end, but they prefer to travel an hour or two each day rather than look for somewhere to live closer to their factories or offices—even though they have no intention of changing their place of work for the rest of their lives. Vienna's districts often consist of numerous smaller communities which in the past were separate villages and continue to preserve their individual characteristics. Connoisseurs are therefore inclined to label you not only according to your accent but also according to your home, which may be in the Laimgruben ('Lime Pit') in the Sixth District, the Brillantengrund ('Diamond Ground') in the Seventh, the Kaasgraben ('Cheese Hollow') in the Nineteenth or among the Weissgärber (the 'Linen Bleachers') in the Third. You may marry and move to another part of the town, but even then you'll be inclined to start your conversations with 'Of course I'm really a Döblingerin (or Hietzingerin or Josefstädterin, etc.)', and you may insist to your dying day that you've never felt quite at home in your new surroundings.

Among the major European cities Vienna is still one of the smaller and more manageable ones. The centre really is the centre, and if you go there to do some shopping you'll also be among the historic sights, and find the opera and theatres and government offices there too. Vienna has never been a great industrial city nor yet a really important commercial one. Its character has been moulded by the fact that for centuries it was an imperial residence and the headquarters of a huge European empire with a markedly centralized bureaucracy. It sounds incredible, but although hotels are sprouting freely all over the town the number of beds available to tourists now is not so large as in the years before the First World War. In those days it was not the tourists from the West but the Austrian citizens from the East who needed accommodation. The administration of the entire Austro-Hungarian Empire was in Vienna, and innumerable officials, soldiers and civil servants came from Bohemia or Hungary, Italy or Yugoslavia to make reports or receive instructions. Many peasants and artisans, workers and intellectuals, came to settle in

Vienna at that time, and from those days date the drab, musty houses, the so-called Zinskasernen ('Rent Barracks') built solidly but squalidly to provide lodging for these immigrants. To a peasant from the depths of Bohemia, used to fetching water from the village well, running water—even if it were only a tap on the landing—seemed luxury, and so did the fact that his home consisted of two separate rooms. By today's standards these flats are wellnigh uninhabitable, but even so it will be a long time before they have been replaced and before that large proportion of the Viennese population that still has no bathroom will be provided with one.

There is still almost no heavy industry in Vienna, and the workers who are about in the early hours of the morning during the week are mostly employed in a variety of lighter industries, such as chemical and pharmaceutical works, radio and television factories or in fancy goods, leatherware or clothing industries. Of course there are also the municipal gas and electricity works, not to mention the Vienna Transport Board—always with too few employees and a whacking deficit at the end of the year. There are sailors too, for although the sea is far away the Danube is navigable, and now that the countries behind the Iron Curtain are becoming interested once more in raising their standard of living, river trips down to the Black Sea are increasing from year to year.

'But where's the Danube?' many visitors ask, after having been in Vienna for some days without having caught sight of it. Vienna does lie on both sides of the river, but unlike Budapest, where the Danube runs through the heart of the city, only small parts of it, the Twenty-first and Twenty-second Districts, lie across its banks. The Reichsbrücke, one of the chief bridges across the Danube, is easily reached from the centre of the city. After the war it was given the name Brücke der Roten Armee ('Bridge of the Red Army'), a name which since the signing of the Austrian Peace Treaty has been completely lost, like other Russianized names such as Tolbuchin Strasse or Stalin Platz. From here one

can see not only the Danube itself, wide and majestic, yet flowing
so swiftly that the tugs and barges have hard work to make their
way upriver, but also the ever growing suburbs on the other side,
new communities and residential zones growing up parallel with
the new industries for which the flat land on that side of the river
is proving so attractive. In 1964 a huge international flower show
was held in a newly laid out park—the Donau Park—just across
the Reichsbrücke, and its symbol the Donauturm, a monstrous
concrete tower topped with rotating restaurant and television
mast, remains, together with stretches of greenery, garden restaurants and an open-air bandstand built on a platform jutting into a
charming lake. This park is likely to become a favourite Viennese
haunt, and when the trees and shrubberies are fully grown may
one day rival the Prater. Among its attractions are the large parking
lots provided at the various entrances.

Motor-cars, as everywhere else in the Western World, are
becoming the menace of the age and the bugbear of the city
authorities. The narrow streets of the inner city are chock-a-block
most of the day: the weary motorist trying to find somewhere to
park is inclined to turn tail and return home without doing his
shopping or whatever he planned to do. There are the so-called
Blue Zones, where parking is permitted for one and a half hours,
and these have helped a little. So far only every sixth Austrian
has a car—but what will happen when the other five have one
also, as no doubt they will as time goes on? The Viennese are not
disciplined drivers. More than half of those taking their tests fail
the first time, and those that do pass do the craziest things. At
the least provocation they forget their famous charm and tap
their heads and roll their eyes to demonstrate what they think of
other people's driving. Subterranean garages are being built
wherever possible, but it is no easy task since many of the older
Viennese houses have two or more storeys below street level.
Various banks have opened drive-in branches in these, while a
well-known department store in the city centre runs a bus service
for motorists who are willing to leave their cars beyond the

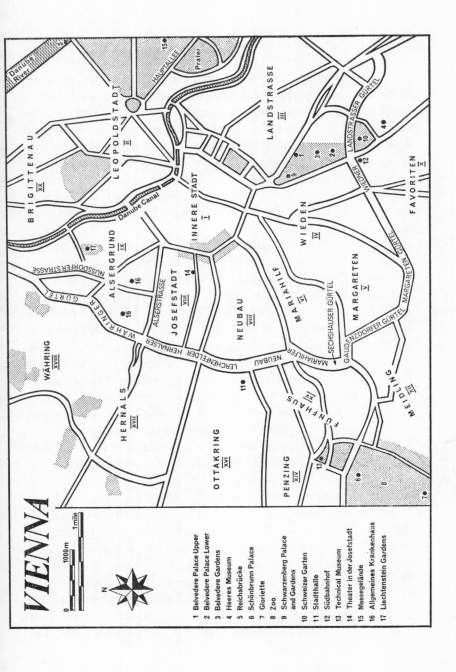

VIENNA

0   1000m   1 mile

N

1 Belvedere Palace Upper
2 Belvedere Palace Lower
3 Belvedere Gardens
4 Heeres Museum
5 Reichsbrücke
6 Schönbrunn Palace
7 Gloriette
8 Zoo
9 Schwarzenberg Palace
   and Gardens
10 Schweizer Garten
11 Stadthalle
12 Südbahnhof
13 Technical Museum
14 Theater in der Josefstadt
15 Messegelände
16 Allgemeines Krankenhaus
17 Liechtenstein Gardens

Danube River

HAUPTALLEE

Prater

BRIGITTENAU
XX

LEOPOLDSTADT
II

LANDSTRASSE
III

LANDSTRASSER GÜRTEL

Danube Canal

INNERE STADT
I

NUSSDORFER STRASSE

ALSERGRUND
IX

WÄHRINGER GÜRTEL

JOSEFSTADT
VIII

ALSERSTRASSE

LERCHENFELDER

HERNALSER

WÄHRING
XVIII

HERNALS
XVII

OTTAKRING
XVI

NEUBAU
VII

NEUBAU

MARIAHILF
VI

WIEDEN
IV

WIEDNER

FAVORITEN
X

MARGARETEN
V

MARGARETEN GÜRTEL

SECHSHAUSER GÜRTEL

GAUDENZDORFER GÜRTEL

MARIAHILFER

FÜNFHAUS
XV

PENZING
XIV

MEIDLING
XII

Ringstrasse, which still encloses most of the actual city. Every year or so the question of whether the streets around St Stephen's at least should be barred to motor traffic is discussed, but it would be a hardship for the many people still living there if they had to walk for miles before being able to get into their own cars. Unlike London or New York there are no purely business districts in Vienna. The upper floors of most office or commercial buildings consist of flats, and blocks of flats continue to be built even in the city centre, because many Viennese, used to living here from childhood, refuse to let themselves be banished to residential areas or the suburbs.

The wave of mechanization cannot be held back, neither can the wave of Americanization rolling across the city. Someone once said that the real victor in the last war was the manufacturer of Coca-Cola, and there is some truth in it. Vienna has always been famous for its little shops, and compared with many other western cities a lot of them still exist. Department stores are a rarity, but self-service stores, discount stores, shopping centres, are all mushrooming throughout the city. More women go to work in Vienna than in any other western European city, and so their shopping has to be done quickly and as close to their homes or working places as possible. Housewives who can afford to be just that still go to the many markets. Now that refrigerators are no longer a luxury but a household necessity and make the storage of food possible for days on end, it is just a question of finding a parking place close enough to your house to enable you to unload so that your trip to the market was worth while. The most famous market is the Naschmarkt in the Fifth District, the cheapest the Brunnenmarkt in the Sixteenth. There are also so-called *Markthallen*, covered markets, and the best known of these is in the Third District, where a vegetable, fruit and grocery market stands opposite the meat market. Prices here are often as much as 25 per cent below those in the butchers' shops in residential areas, and thrifty housewives from all over the town come and do their shopping here. There is of course no comparison between this meat market and, say, Les

Halles in Paris, but some of the market helpers seem to be characters straight out of a comic film, their jovial faces, bleary-eyed and red and dominated by multicoloured bulbous noses, testifying to many icy mornings spent in the pub across the way. Here a notice categorically states that only market helpers are served between the hours of 2 a.m. and 6 a.m.

The school child's day, like the office worker's, starts at 8 a.m., but after lunch, except for homework, the day is his own. As the years go on each child comes home at a different time, wants to be fed at all hours and needs help of some sort with its homework in the afternoon. But the very concentrated school work in the early hours has much to be said for it. The teachers believe that between 8 a.m. and 11 a.m. a child can take in twice as much as later on in the day. Games play only a very minor part in school life in Vienna; many schools have not as much as a courtyard for outdoor games, but swimming and gym are obligatory and there is a fortnight's skiing for children in secondary schools.

Most schools are in fact rather dreary barracks, enveloped in their own peculiar odour of chalk and ink and oiled floors. They are, one feels, built for hard work and nothing else. The human side of learning seems to be missing, not only in the school system but also, later on, in the universities, and this lack is made up for only by the excellence of many of the teachers themselves.

The Anglo-American college system is completely unknown in Austria. After nine years of secondary education and with the *Matura* certificate in your hand you can make for a place of higher learning, but once again most of the student's time will be spent at home or on the way to and from the university or academy where he studies.

Vienna has a very high reputation for learning, and it is surprising that under present conditions—lack of space, lack of teachers, lack of modern facilities and, of course, lack of funds—this reputation is still alive. Many students come to Vienna, particularly from the Near East and eastern Europe, and how to

house them all, as well as the large number of students from
the provinces, is one of the Ministry of Education's problems.
Various hostels have been built, landladies are begged and bullied
into letting their rooms at reasonable prices—which means about
S.600 a month for a passable room, exclusive of heating—but
the idea of a college campus or *cité université* is gaining support.
Universities are being built in Linz and Salzburg and this decen-
tralization may also help to solve the problem. In the meantime
students at the Technical University who want to hear and see
properly must often queue up in the early hours of the morning
in order to get a good seat in the lecture hall, and latecomers are
simply turned away, while at the University the problem of
laboratory space seems to be becoming insurmountable. So far
student life in Vienna is negligible. Around the University and
the various academies clusters of young people can be seen.
Certain cafés and pubs are frequented by them—the university
canteen, though very cheap, is pretty terrible—but on the whole,
once the lecture is over, once the day's experiments are finished,
students become submerged in their families or, if they are
away from home, in an anonymous and often rather lonely
background.

Anonymity is one of the advantages of great cities. In London
or New York one feels as free as a bird—no one need know you,
no one will bother even if you decide to jump over the moon. In
Vienna today there is still only a certain degree of this anonymity.
The city cannot compare in size with many of its sisters, and
while the fact that 'up town' is concentrated within so small
an area is in some ways an advantage it can also be a decided
disadvantage. Before the war one of the most frequented cafés
was the Kaffee Fenstergucker ('Spy at the Window', one might
translate this) in the Kärntnerstrasse which, alas, was bombed out.
It used to be said that if you sat there long enough all your
friends would in time pass by. Vienna really is a very difficult
place in which to escape either friend or foe.

Between the routine of 'early to rise' and 'early to bed',

which to most people's surprise is also a Viennese characteristic, there is a hard day's work for most people, but with frequent pleasant intervals for meals. At nine o'clock a roll and sausage, at eleven a glass of beer (or even Coca-Cola). Lunch time itself in both office and factory does not last much longer than half an hour. There is a canteen to go to, a lunch box to open or a *Gasthaus* just round the corner to pop into. Tea shops like Lyons' are quite unknown here. Cheap food, often passably well and sometimes even excellently cooked, is to be had in innumerable *Gasthäuser*. These sometimes look fairly forbidding from the outside—old-fashioned and with no frills. Inside the atmosphere is smoke-beer-and-goulash laden, but the menus are often incredibly cheap and even a meal *à la carte* doesn't cost much. The service is usually quick and good, because, as I say, lunch time for most workers is very limited, so if you are in a hurry for a cheap meal, don't be put off by too much local colour: there'll always be a friendly welcome for you in the humblest café.

Night life in Vienna is strictly for tourists—or so it seems. The Viennese, the solid citizens, go to the theatre or to a concert, but these start around seven o'clock and are over by ten, and after that, unless one goes out for a meal, one just goes home—to bed. The bars and cabarets are exactly the same as anywhere else, and there are just one or two where the younger Viennese set can be found. But on the whole once ten o'clock is past Viennese streets are fairly quiet and after eleven very quiet. At midnight even the street lamps become dim and only waiters hurrying home, street cleaners wielding their long brooms and a few stragglers having frankfurters with mustard at a coffee stall seem still to be about.

I have often wondered why I prefer living in Vienna to any-where else. There are no major differences in everyday life from that of any other large European city. There are other cities which are larger, more lively and even more beautiful. And yet, when I've been away for any length of time, I long to get back. Perhaps the reason is that in Vienna even with fairly little money

B

you can still live your own life without having to try to keep up
with the Müllers. Mass society has not submerged the individual
entirely. How long will it stay that way? How long will it be
before deep frozen, ready-to-eat menus replace the homely
Apfelstrudel and goulash, drive-in stores finally force the small
grocers to capitulate and canned music stifles the memory of the
sweet familiar tunes of violin and accordion at a *Heurigen*?

From the possible Vienna of the future, let us turn back to a
little of the city's rich past, which helps so much our understanding and enjoyment of the present.

Chapter 2

Bulwark between East and West

AT THE back of the church Zu den sieben Chören der Engel ('To the Seven Angelic Choirs'), which stands on Am Hof, one of Vienna's oldest squares, there is a confusion of narrow, twisting streets, and tiny ramshackle shops nestle between its buttresses. At night, when the booming traffic seems far away, and the steep roof of the Gothic choir stands stark against the sky, it is not difficult to imagine the sound of horses' hoofs on the cobbled streets or a richly dressed burgher emerging from one of the narrow-fronted, slightly lopsided houses which still stand here.

Over at the Belvedere Palace, as the moonlight slides across the baroque perfection of buildings and gardens, now mirrored in the ornamental waters of the lake, now atomized in the fountains' sparkling spray, the ghosts are of elegants in wigs and silk gowns, of gilt carriages and torch-bearers, harpsichords and minuets.

In the Innere Burghof, the courtyard within the Imperial Palace which is surrounded by buildings dating from many reigns, many centuries, we may recall the utter blackness and solemnity of an imperial funeral procession, perhaps that of the Emperor Francis Joseph: black horses, black plumes, top hats and veils, against the red and gold cipher above the Schweizertor. Not only an emperor but an empire is dead.

Everywhere in Vienna history is alive; it can no more be ignored than can those features of modern life which it has in common with other cities—traffic jams, skyscrapers, haste and noise.

The history of Vienna as a city does not go back so far as that of many other great cities, though settlements are known to have existed in this area as early as 5000 B.C. Look at a map and it is not difficult to see why. The Vienna Basin is an ideal place for a settlement. First, there is the Danube, one of Europe's mightiest rivers, serving both as a protection and a thoroughfare eastward through central Europe. There, to the north and west, lie the last foothills of the Alps, the sheltering Kahlenberg, Leopoldsberg and Bisamberg. Farther down the river there is the Hainburger Pforte, the perfect natural fortification towards the east. Meteorologists and geologists vie with each other in describing the rich variety which the Vienna Basin offers. It is the mixture of Alpine ruggedness, streams and meadows and wide plains, coupled with that enormous climatic span between harsh mountain winds and the dry enervating heat of the Pannonian flatlands, which has always characterized Vienna.

But it was not mere rhetoric when Metternich said that Asia lay directly beyond Vienna, for the situation of the city, however favourable from a local point of view, is by European standards that of an outpost. The West, to which it has always belonged by culture, history and tradition, comes to an end here: Vienna is and always has been its final bastion. Always its role has been that of bulwark, gateway or mediatrix. It reminds one of a seaport: exposed to the coming and going of people from all parts of the world, it is filled with the same zest for life, the same kind of ever-changing population.

It was not until the Roman conquest of Vienna in 15 B.C. that the city began to have an important place on the map of Europe. Just beyond St Stephen's Cathedral is a little museum, open to the public, which contains relics of the Roman occupation, which were discovered after the Second World War when the rubble left by innumerable bombing attacks had been cleared away. After the Romans left, in A.D. 400, it was centuries before the modern city began to take shape. Its medieval appearance is shown in the paintings of the unknown 'Meister des Schottenstiftes', dating from about 1475, which are in the possession of

the Benedictine 'Schotten' monastery. The artist used Vienna
as a background for such biblical scenes as the 'Flight into Egypt'
and the 'Visitation', which contain portraits of the Kärntnerstrasse and of the skyline of the Inner City still perfectly recognizable today. The name of the monastery derives, oddly enough,
from the importation of monks from Ireland; the community
was labelled 'Scots' even after it had been replaced by German
brethren.

This identification of the modern city with a medieval pattern
is not so surprising when it is remembered that the walls and
fortifications raised by Duke Leopold VI in the early years of the
thirteenth century remained intact, and contained the greater
part of the city until the Emperor Francis Joseph had them razed
in 1860 in order to build the Ringstrasse. Leopold's city, which
in those days consisted mostly of clusters of houses here and there
among vineyards and gardens, was surrounded by walls which
must have appeared to his citizens as at least three sizes too large.
Today the broad boulevard merely encloses the First District.

And so, here and there, traces of medieval Vienna linger on,
as in the narrow crooked streets around the lovely Gothic church
of Maria am Gestade. The church's name means 'St Mary's on
the Shore', for an arm of the Danube once flowed here, and it was
a sailors' and fishermen's church, which first rose in the shape of a
poor wooden building, to be replaced in the fourteenth century
by this narrow, high-shouldered structure which is reported to
have taken two hundred years to build. The houses round it,
some of them flanking on one side the broad stairs leading up to
its façade, are very old. In the 1930's a number of them were
demolished to provide a better view of the church, and during
the Second World War many more were destroyed by bombing.

The oldest house in Vienna is not easy to find. It stands in the
Griechengassl, which leads from the Fleischmarkt down to the
Franz-Josefs Kai. This is not only one of the oldest parts of Vienna
but also the most oriental. The Greek colony, for centuries con-
sisting of carpet and spice merchants, is still housed here, every

second shop seems to have carpets on show, and the Greek
Orthodox Church rubs shoulders with its fellow of the Catholic
Eastern Rite. The Griechengassl itself, a steep cobbled thoroughfare which hardly merits the description 'street', still bears a black
and white weatherbeaten sign from the year 1912, on which is
inscribed: 'PEDESTRIANS: BEWARE OF HORSE-DRAWN VEHICLES.
WALKING PACE ONLY ALLOWED! DRIVERS OF HEAVY VEHICLES
MUST LEAD THEIR HORSES BY THE REINS OR MUST SEND AN ADULT
PERSON AHEAD TO WARN PEDESTRIANS.' One almost listens for the
clatter of hoofs and the cries of drivers as they manage this
ticklish bit of manœuvring.

No. 7 in the Griechengassl is a single-storeyed building, its
façade decorated with a baroque Madonna and a handsome
lantern, so that at first sight the house does not strike one as
being unusually old. But once inside its antiquity is convincing.
Everything is dim and sombre: the round windows, the boxed-in
stairs and the quiet, crooked courtyard, with its Gothic buttresses
supporting a tower-like building next door. The Danube used to
flow just beneath, but today only an artificial arm of the river,
subdued into the Danube Canal and lacking even a shimmer of
romance, hurries along to rejoin the Danube proper where, just
below the city, Vienna's port used to be. Here too, over the way,
is one of Vienna's oldest inns, the Griechenbeisl, dark and
dank, one narrow panelled parlour leading into the next, the
thick stench of beer and goulash impregnating every passageway
and corner. The inn now attracts so many tourists that its atmosphere is largely destroyed.

And yet it is not difficult to imagine that it was here that the
Liebe Augustin, a fickle, worthless and probably mostly tipsy
bagpipe-player, started on his way to fame. For the Viennese he
exemplifies that sense of resignation coupled with self-irony,
humour and *sang-froid* which they secretly admire and outwardly
deplore in themselves, and which later led to the birth of the
aphorism: 'In Berlin the situation is serious but not hopeless;
in Vienna the situation is hopeless, but not serious.' Augustin

himself, so the story goes (although scholars are now inclined
to believe that he never really existed), spent his days in roving
from one inn to the next to sample the wine and beer. This he
continued to do even while the plague was raging in 1679, and
one evening his unsteady path led straight into a common grave
already full of corpses. Here he spent a restful night, and next
morning drew attention with his bagpipe melodies to his living
self, so that some courageous citizens pulled him out and saved
him. He was unscathed, and his favourite ditty:

> Oh, Du lieber Augustin,
> Alles ist hin . . .

about everything being gone, including money and man and
proud Vienna itself, while he must lie in the mud, became as
closely associated with Vienna as 'Oranges and Lemons' is with
London.

All this happened long after the passing of medieval Vienna
and long after the Hapsburgs were making Vienna irrevocably
their city.

The fortifications were largely paid for by the huge sums
demanded from the English by Duke Leopold of Austria as
ransom for Richard Cœur de Lion. In fact the ransom paid not
only for building the fortifications of Vienna but for those of
three other Austrian cities, although the Pope on a number of
occasions threatened Leopold with excommunication if he did
not repay the money, since it was illegal to take prisoner anyone
returning from the Holy Wars.

Many streets in the centre of Vienna are reminders that by the
early thirteenth century it was no mere ducal residence, but had
developed into a lively and flourishing city of burghers and
artisans, second only to Cologne, so Leopold VI assures the Pope
in a letter of that time. In the Wollzeile the wool merchants had
their shops, and not far away in the Bäckerstrasse and Fleischmarkt bakers and butchers were at home. A little farther on, past
the Neue Markt, is the Tuchlauben, where cloth merchants

VIENNA

N

0 500m
½ mile

AUGARTEN

Danube Canal

FRANZ JOSEFS KAI

Maria am Gestade Church

Ruprechtskirche

Altes Rathaus

SCHOTTEN RING

WIPPLINGERSTRASSE

Schotten Monastery

AM HOF

FREYUNG

Harrach Palais

DR KLUEGER RING

SCHWARZSPANIERSTRASSE

University

Rathaus Park

spread their wares under Gothic arches. This street leads straight
into the Kohlmarkt, or coal market, where coal could once be
bought, but which is now one of Vienna's smartest shopping
streets.

Not only trade but the Church flourished. St Leopold III
helped to establish monasteries such as those of the Cistercians at
Heiligenkreuz and the Augustinian Canons at Klosterneuburg.
The latter was his very own and favourite foundation, and he
now lies buried beneath what is perhaps Austria's greatest
artistic treasure, the Verdun Altar. The brilliance of its gold and
enamel panels, on which are depicted scenes from the Bible,
is almost startling when the lights are suddenly turned on in the
gloomy crypt. Each little scene and each ornament seems perfection. The enamelling technique which Master Nicholas of Verdun
developed has never been equalled.

Centuries later the Emperor Charles VI was to be as closely
attached to Klosterneuburg as Leopold, and he planned to extend
it into a sort of Austrian Escorial, part monastery, part imperial
palace. As with so many projects the Hapsburgs undertook it was
never fully realized and only two of the four wings of the palace
were built.

The Deutsches Haus, home of the Teutonic Knights, stands
behind St Stephen's, just where it stood at its foundation in 1210.
The small, intimate church of St Elisabeth incorporated in it is
one of the few Gothic buildings which have remained unchanged,
and was untouched during baroque times. Lighted only with
candles flickering gently in the many chandeliers, and with muted
daylight falling through the narrow windows along one side of
the church, this is one of the most charming settings for a wedding
in Vienna that I know, though all too many people continue to
dream of a wedding in the Hofburgkapelle, the Imperial Chapel,
where members of the royal family used to marry but where
today anyone willing to make application to the proper authorities
can do so.

For two features more closely linked with Viennese history

than any others we have to thank the first remarkable Hapsburg, Rudolf IV, who came to the throne in 1358 at the age of nineteen. In 1365, shortly before his death, he founded the University, the second oldest German language university on the Continent. More important still, he had given orders for the planning and building of the Gothic version of St Stephen's Cathedral, and although it was not to be completed for two centuries it was built according to the plans approved by him.

Who was the actual architect of the most deeply loved symbol of Vienna we do not know. The names of many masons are inscribed in its stones, but innumerable legends are associated with this magnificent Gothic church. What is fact is that here is a building which embodies everything Vienna stands for, which has shared its history throughout the centuries, and whose tower, 'der alte Steffl', as it is popularly known, is perhaps the finest Gothic spire in the world. Tapering gently upward, it is 450 feet from its massive base to its airy pinnacle.

Why it is St Stephen's and not another church that has played such an important part in the life of Vienna is not clear. It is by no means Vienna's oldest church—the Ruprechtskirche and the original Peterskirche are both much older—and when the first, Romanesque, building was raised in 1137–47 it stood beyond the city walls. But from the moment of its conception the parish church of St Stephen's took a special place in the development of the town, and soon it was difficult to think of Vienna without this remarkable, ever-growing and ever-changing church.

It is characteristic of the city, conservative in all things, that it was loath to destroy the original Romanesque building when the larger Gothic church was begun, and so that first happy marriage of styles which makes St Stephen's what it is was achieved. The Romanesque west front with its imposing *Riesentor*, rich in symbols and traditional ornaments, and the two west towers, the so-called *Heidentürme*, were retained, and slowly the Gothic choir and triple nave rose beyond them. Long before the vaulting of these was completed the south tower had risen to its full height, and from the year of its completion, 1433, to the present day, this delicately wrought marvel of Gothic craftsmanship has kept a watchful eye on the ever-spreading city below it. The second spire, that of the north tower, was never to be completed. Lack of funds led to its crowning with a stocky turret topped with a baroque onion roof—which sounds impossible but actually appears perfectly congruous.

Legend of course would have it that the devil was responsible and would not permit the spire's completion. But, as I have said, the legends about St Stephen's are innumerable, and angels and devils are held responsible for all sorts of odd happenings. Perhaps the oddest legends are those centred round the bowling alley—the smallest in the world—which, according to tradition rather than fact, was to be found in the watch-keeper's room. One watch-keeper prided himself on always being able to knock over all the nine skittles, and was greatly annoyed when an old man one day appeared in his room and offered to take him on. To make sure that he would not be beaten he threw one of the nine skittles out of the window. But the old man, who was none other than Death, croaked, 'Ah, but even if there are only eight of them, I'll get nine, all told', and knocked over the watch-keeper himself, who fell dead at his feet. He is said still to haunt the tower, where he is for ever seeking the missing skittle.

The Gothic church was to be building for over two hundred years, but the result justified all expectations. Unlike Gothic cathedrals in western Europe St Stephen's is not a basilica, with a high central nave flanked on each side by slightly lower aisles. Instead a magnificent, towering, almost hunchbacked roof spreads over all three aisles, only the roof covering the choir being separate and somewhat lower.

This great roof is as much of a symbol as is the tower itself. Early paintings and engravings of the church show that the original Gothic roof was covered with the same maze of brilliantly coloured glazed tiles, forming zigzag patterns, as they do today. This gaudy richness is at first an astonishing sight, and yet the idea that it is intended to represent the carpet of the East, the Orient's most sacred symbol, as opposed to the spire, typical of Western, Catholic thought, seems remarkably logical. Vienna has always stood where East and West meet, and St Stephen's was meant to face in both directions.

While the foundations and early origin of St Stephen's are due to the generosity and interest of princes, its later development and completion were very much in the hands of the townspeople. During the Renaissance and baroque epochs additions rather than major changes were made, but these additions, of oratories, tombstones and altars, were in such good taste that they did not impinge on the existing Gothic perfection; nowhere perhaps can such a complete and happy assimilation of styles be found as here, where the baroque high altar does not seem inapt in front of the brilliant colours of Gothic stained glass, or the numerous smaller side altars out of place beneath soaring Gothic pillars.

No one who enters the cathedral today can possibly imagine what it looked like in 1945, when it was completely gutted and seemingly irrevocably lost to posterity. Incendiary bombs and shelling had set the roof on fire, and the larch girders—an entire forest of larches is said to have been used—had collapsed, and the whole roof had crashed through the vaulting on to the floor below. The place was a terrible, tragic sight. From the ashes has emerged a new St Stephen's, different in small details but on the whole unchanged.

Of many details in St Stephen's dear to the hearts not only of art historians but of every Viennese, it is perhaps the two images of Anton Pilgram which attract most curiosity. Pilgram was one of the most gifted, but at the same time personally less admirable, masons who worked on St Stephen's. The chancel is his work, but this superb masterpiece was not sufficient glory for him: he wanted a more personal monument to his own greatness. So at the foot of the chancel, and again at the foot of the organ loft in the left aisle, he peers out, coolly self possessed, even a little disgruntled. The pulpit itself, dating from about 1512, is a wonderful

piece of carving in mellow sandstone. The heads of popes and
bishops which decorate it are full of life, the ornaments are rich
and original. The staircase winding its elegant way upwards bears
on its banisters an odd assembly of frogs and lizards, scurrying
up and down in apparent fear and amazement. There have been
many explanations for the presence of these strange creatures, the
most likely being that the frog, which in Gothic times was a
symbol of evil, is being attacked by the lizards which, always
seeking the light, were the symbols of righteousness, just as
God's word preached from the pulpit attacks sin and evil. The
pulpit nowadays looks slightly naked, since at the restoration of
the cathedral it was discovered that its roof was actually the lid
of the baptismal font, so it was returned to its proper place.

The one memorial to the artistic patronage of the Emperor
Maximilian in Vienna is the Hofburgkapelle, to which is attached
the world famous Vienna Boys' Choir. Some of the boys spend
much of their time touring other countries, while others sing at
Mass in the Hofburgkapelle each Sunday.

Some of the city's finest buildings arose as a result of the Court's
urgent need in the sixteenth century to find lodgings for its ever-
increasing staff. The Imperial Palace, the Hofburg, began slowly
and erratically to be enlarged. Various wings, at first the Leopold-
inische Trakt and later the Amalien Trakt, were built, while in
1552 the so-called 'Schweizertor', leading from the Innere
Burghof to the Schweizerhof, was erected. This is the finest
Renaissance archway, and indeed monument, remaining in the
city today, its simple nobility unimpaired by later alterations.
Through it many thousands of people continue to pass on their
way to the Hofburgkapelle and the Schatzkammer, the former
Imperial Treasury, which lie beyond. The nobility too began to
build, but only very few of the palaces erected about that time
remain and these seem somehow *gauche*: they are built according
to theories and rules but lack the instinctive perfection which
characterized the later baroque palaces.

The defeat of the Turks in 1686 when, for the second time in less than 150 years they besieged Vienna, not only made it the centre of attraction for all Christendom but set the seal on its emergence as the Imperial City *par excellence*. In the Heeresmuseum, a very fine army museum, are some of the trophies which the fleeing Turks left behind when, after a Viennese garrison of 16,000 had held out for two months against an enemy of 230,000, the besiegers were routed by Prince Charles of Lorraine and King John Sobieski of Poland. The exhibits include richly ornamented tents, silken cushions, frightful swords and the famous horsetails which the Turks bore before them in battle. From the guns left behind the great bell of St Stephen's, the *Pummering*, was cast. On the Freyung, at the corner of the Strauchgasse, the figure of a Turk on horseback, his sabre held high, occupies a niche in the wall of a house. This is the so-called Heidenschuss, and again the legends associated with the statue are many. Turkish cannon balls are still lodged in the walls of some of the houses in the centre of the city, among them the *Gasthaus* 'Zum güldenen Drachen' in the Steindlgasse, a very old and charming establishment.

Charles VI and his daughter Maria Theresa are associated with much of Vienna's finest baroque, and it was during their reigns that the greatest changes took place in the city. Joseph II, who followed his mother to the throne, was full of ideas for a new and modern world. He abhorred pomp and circumstance and saw himself merely as his people's servant, dreaming of freedom for all men. As is so often the case with men far ahead of their age, he was able to do little good for either himself or his city. Some of his institutions, such as the Allgemeines Krankenhaus, the General Hospital, were amazingly modern—even today the buildings are still in use, and though now of course they are rather unpractical their layout and planning must have been revolutionary for their time.

Napoleon's victorious campaigns throughout Europe stirred up Vienna. At Aspern, just outside the city, he suffered his first defeat on land through the Archduke Charles, but the Austrian

victory came to nothing when Napoleon triumphed shortly
afterwards at Kagran. On the Heldenplatz the magnificent
equestrian statue of the Archduke, his horse fiercely rearing and
he himself holding aloft the Austrian standard, bears witness to
the Aspern victory. The Archduke himself, a brilliant, shy and
slight man, was more than sceptical when he saw early paintings
of the scene. 'Why,' he admonished his admirers, 'with my being
the size I am, how could I possibly have carried that huge flag
around with me, not to mention lifting it up above my head!'

The long reign of Francis Joseph, who came to the throne in
1848 as an intelligent and comely youth of eighteen, meant for
Vienna a second flowering. In its baroque age it had become an
imperial city; now it became a modern metropolis. Anyone who
lived at least part of his life during that reign remembers it with
nostalgia. There were wars, there were losses and tragedies, but
life generally was still orderly, comfortable and serene. Francis
Joseph symbolized the very spirit of his times, and with his going
in 1916 not only an era but a mode of life was gone also.

Only a plaque in the Kaisergruft commemorates the last
emperor, Charles, who was obliged to abandon the throne in
1918 and who died in Madeira in 1922.

The years between the two wars were for Vienna years of
political unrest and economic uncertainty. But even so she could
boast of social institutions, particularly workers' flats, which
were to be unrivalled in Europe for many years. The huge Karl
Marx Hof in Heiligenstadt, which is more than a kilometre in
length, was the largest municipal dwelling erected anywhere in
Europe at that time. Today it appears almost like a fortress; the
bright blues and reds and yellows of its various blocks, the arches
and battlements, seem to represent might rather than comfort,
and indeed it still bears the marks of shelling when, during the
political skirmishes of 1934, it was besieged.

During the Nazi era the face of Vienna changed little. By the
end of the Second World War the changes were terrible and
seemingly irreparable. It was only during the latter years of the

THE PULPIT IN ST STEPHEN'S CATHEDRAL ... a portrait of its creator, Master Pilgram, looks out from beneath heads of popes and bishops full of life; ornaments rich and original (*page 21*)

STEPHEN'S CATHEDRAL
s shared Vienna's history
roughout the centuries
(page 19)

HE KARL MARX HOF (left),
the thirties the largest
orkers' flats in Europe
age 24) and ...

THE GRIECHENGASSL,
one of the oldest parts
of Vienna (page 13) ...

A REMINDER OF THE TURKISH SIEGE
of 1683, on the Freyung
(page 23)

Bis zum J. 1456
floß durch diese Gasse
und durch den tiefen Graben

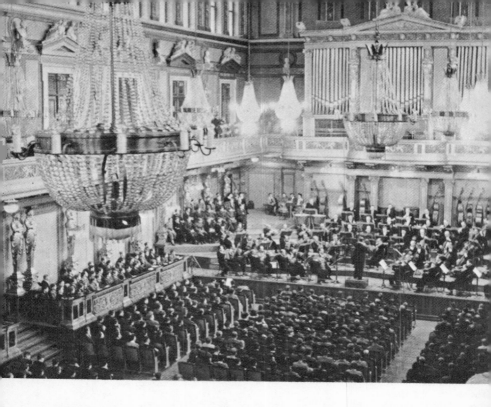

'A GOLDEN TEMPLE OF SOUND', the concert hall of the Society of
Friends of Music, which numbered Beethoven, Schubert and
Brahms among its members and has existed for a hundred and fifty years (*page 27*)

IN A GARRET OF THE HOUSE ON THE LEFT CORNER of
Michaelerplatz Haydn was studying music at the age of nineteen (*page 29*)

THE DOMGASSE.
In one of these houses Mozart
composed *The Magic Flute*

IN HEILIGENSTADT, one of the many 'Beethoven houses' in the city

'THE PALACE OF SCHÖNBRUNN still breathes life, perhaps because it lives on in the affections of the Viennese' (pages 40–1)

THE PESTSAÜLE ON THE GRABEN
'. . . a mixture of theatrical hyperbole, fervent faith and joyous rapture' (*page 37*)

THE DOME OF THE KARLSKIRCHE, a brilliant green,
can be seen all over Vienna (*page 38*)

war that large-scale daylight bombing took place, but the final destruction was proportionately as extensive as that of London, and Vienna being so much smaller the resulting chaos was all the more noticeable. Finally, during the battle of Vienna in April 1945, the city was pounded until nothing seemed to remain except smoking mounds of rubble.

The early post-war years were as gloomy as those that followed the First World War. And yet there was a difference. For the first time there was a feeling of self-confidence in the air, self-confidence in Austria's, in Vienna's, ability to rise again, to find itself. The typical Viennese attitude of 'Da muss was g'schehn' ('Something must be done about it') was not followed by the equally classic corollary 'Da kann man halt nix machen' ('There's nothing we can do about it'). Something was done. The heaps of rubble disappeared. Bread might be a luxury but music wasn't, and the Vienna Philharmonics played to packed houses. It did not seem to matter that one had to walk for miles on an empty stomach to be able to hear them. The Opera was destroyed, but operatic performances were put on almost as soon as the fighting in Vienna itself was over, and the Theater an der Wien was taken over for that purpose. Vienna was a city divided into four allied zones, but nowhere in the world were these four to be on such amicable terms as here. Once again Vienna was the easternmost bulwark of the Western world. Without apparent courage, but rather with that mixture of lackadaisical charm and an imbued feeling for East-West relations, Vienna managed to hold its own.

From the moment the Austrian State Treaty was signed in May 1955 life in Vienna changed radically. The treaty, which no one had dared to hope for but which had been so deeply desired, established definitely the fact that Vienna belonged to the West, and as soon as it was no longer in the Russian Zone tourists from all over the world came once again to visit the lovely metropolis on the Danube.

The 'Economic Miracle', so much admired in Germany, spread to Austria, so that the trend continues to be upward and

C

Vienna is experiencing a renewed blossoming. But even this economic upswing is not taken entirely seriously by the Viennese, whose comment on it is: 'In Germany the economic miracle is the result of planning, hard work, investment, thoroughness, application, industrial leadership and so on. In Austria—why, the economic miracle really is a miracle.'

In Vienna, of course, miracles have happened before. Some of them are almost forgotten, others remain alive and visible. The greatest miracle can be heard rather than seen. It is the flow of music that for centuries has coursed through the city and has left a unique impression on it. In Vienna there really does seem to be music in the air.

Chapter 3

There's Music in the Air

VIENNA and music are inseparable. Music flows through the city, and the visitor can hear it in the churches and concert halls, and even along the streets where lavender women still cry their wares.

The Society of Friends of Music has existed for 150 years, and has included amongst its honorary members Beethoven, Schubert and Brahms. Its concert hall, the opulent Grosse Musikvereinssaal, a golden temple of sound, with the Five Graces sweeping across the ceiling in glowing colours and with its huge sparkling chandeliers, has been named their favourite concert hall by some of the world's most famous conductors.

Whether Vienna itself would awaken similar happy memories is more doubtful. Famous the world over as the birthplace of so much great music, it has nevertheless not always been entirely kind to musicians of genius. The innate conservatism which in Vienna dominates all the arts has often rejected anything new or revolutionary, so that some of her greatest sons were acclaimed only after a hard life and bitter death.

No one would have thought that this was to be Wolferl Mozart's fate when he first arrived in Vienna from Salzburg in 1762. Just six years old, he was accompanied by his father and sister, and had been commanded to perform before the Empress Maria Theresa and her family at Schönbrunn Palace. Delightedly, but also a little deprecatingly, his father was able to report home that his success had been immediate and prodigious, and that after his performance Wolferl had jumped into the Empress's motherly lap and had soundly kissed her. And yet when he died only twenty-nine years later no proper funeral could be arranged for lack of funds, and the few faithful friends who struggled along behind his coffin on a stormy January night, as it left the house in Rauhensteingasse, at the back of St Stephen's, saw it lowered into a common grave from which it was never to be recovered. There is only a monument bearing his name among the graves of other great composers on the Zentralfriedhof, Vienna's main cemetery.

His early childhood success endeared Mozart to the Viennese. The short years of his life were filled to overflowing with music— symphonies, chamber music and operas. Among the last were *The Marriage of Figaro*, composed in the Domgasse, one of the narrow meandering alleys behind St Stephen's, and *The Magic Flute*, the first German *opera buffa*. This, with Mozart himself conducting and with the librettist Schikaneder as Papageno, was a huge success at the Theater an der Wien. Vienna, while ignoring his personal plight, rejoiced in his melodies.

Beethoven's funeral in 1827 was very different. Thousands of people, among them members of the nobility, patrons of the arts, as well as common folk, followed Beethoven's coffin from the Schwarzspanierstrasse to the Weiss-Spanier Church in the Alserstrasse. How many people know that it was only thanks to English generosity that such a funeral was possible? Shortly before his death Beethoven, almost as destitute as Mozart, had written to friends in England and they had sent £100 which had been collected on his behalf. The money did not arrive in time to ease his life, but it provided a worthy setting for his death.

Beethoven came to Vienna in 1792. It was too late for him to see his dearest wish fulfilled, which was to study with Mozart, who had already died, and instead he turned to Haydn and took lessons in composition and counterpoint with him. Why, one wonders, did Beethoven never return to his native Bonn? Vienna seems to have held him. With its people he was never on the easiest of terms, even before deafness drove him ever more into himself, but the city seemed to him the ideal setting for his music. He personally dominated not only Vienna but the entire scene. His leonine head and stocky figure, hands crossed behind his back, his unkempt appearance, became familiar to the Viennese. His music, though sometimes startling and, towards the end, incomprehensible, was both applauded and played. Vienna loves her adopted sons, as she loves anything foreign, and prides herself on assimilating them; but their personal fate, she feels, is not her concern.

Quite apart from his music Beethoven was to leave his mark all over the city. He was a rolling stone, never in one place but he wished to be somewhere else. He moved from one lodging to another, from the centre of the city to the suburbs and back again. There are more houses with the commemorating plaque 'Beethoven lived here' than seems credible. He did not, of course, ingratiate himself with his landlords by scribbling notes on window panes and shutters instead of on paper.

Beethoven had left the service of Prince Max Franz of Cologne when he came to Vienna, and was the first of the classic composers to be able to exist independently, without fixed employment. Mozart's struggles with his master, the Prince Archbishop of Salzburg, had often been bitter; Haydn had been luckier with his patron, Prince Esterházy.

'Papa' Haydn's life was altogether sunnier than either Mozart's or Beethoven's. He has always been loved and cherished unequivocally by the Viennese, perhaps subconsciously delighted that on his account they need have no twinges of conscience.

His beginnings were not as spectacular as Mozart's, whose senior he was by twenty-four years. Born of poor peasant folk in Rohrau in the Burgenland, almost on the present Hungarian border, he came to Vienna at the age of nine as a choirboy, and ten years later was busily studying music in the garret of the house adjoining the Michaelerkirche. After another ten years he was musician at the court of Prince Esterházy in Eisenstadt. Vienna and Eisenstadt were to remain the hub of his world, which he seldom left except for repeated visits to London in the latter part of his life.

In those days Vienna was indeed a musical Mecca, for where else could you find composers such as Mozart, Haydn, Beethoven and Schubert all living in one city within the span of a single generation? A century later Bruckner, Brahms, Hugo Wolf and Mahler, not to mention the Strauss dynasty, were to repeat this golden musical age. Their music belongs to the world, but there is no doubt that of all the composers who lived and worked in Vienna none was more Viennese than Schubert, none more Austrian than Bruckner.

Schubert was born in 1797 in Lichtental, part of today's Ninth District, and he died there in 1828. His whole personality, sunny yet shy, convivial but romantic, mirrored the Vienna of his times. His music is deeply rooted in the folk music and dances of the city, and one cannot imagine his having been born anywhere else. We see him and his friends, the painter Moritz von Schwind, the poët Bauernfeld, the tenor Vogel, strolling through Vienna in the early hours of the morning, accompanying each other home unable to part from each other, often spending the remainder of the night together. And then there were the Schubert evenings, the so-called *Schubertiaden*, with plenty of sparkling wine and Vogel singing Schubert's latest breathtakingly lovely song, with Schubert himself at the piano, his short fat fingers trying to keep up with his own inspiration. Later on he would be persuaded to play some of his waltzes for pretty girls to dance to.

In the Oppolzergasse, opposite the University, stands the delightfully gabled Biedermeier 'Drei Mäderl Haus' where for a time Schubert lived. If it were not a little too reminiscent of that sugary atrocity *Lilac Time*, which adapted Schubert's liveliest melodies into a sickly operetta, it would be the perfect setting for one of these evenings. His birthplace, in the Nussdorferstrasse, is also just as it used to be, a low single-storeyed house, built round an oblong courtyard, with wooden stairs and galleries, twining vines and shady trees.

Two years before his death Schubert was writing a petition to the Emperor Francis I applying for the position of Assistant

Court Conductor, and his humble tone is repeated half a century later by Bruckner during an audience with the Emperor Francis Joseph when, after thanking him for a decoration which had been bestowed upon him, he begged the Emperor to forbid Hanslick, the feared and godlike critic, to write so badly about him. Francis Joseph felt that there was little he could do about this. But what a typical scene in the life of a man so simple as to appear not merely childlike but childish, and yet at the same time a musician greater, more powerful and more original than almost any other Austrian composer.

Bruckner came to Vienna when he was appointed professor at the Conservatory, but his roots remained in his native Upper Austria, in the country around the Augustinian Abbey of St Florian, where he asked to be buried. Bruckner's music, more than any other, is wholly Austrian. Perhaps that is the reason why it has never become as internationally popular as that of his predecessors Mozart and Haydn or his contemporary Brahms. To understand it one must know Austria, its scenery, the mountains and valleys, the rich pastures and dark forests, the baroque churches and solid farmsteads. All these come alive in Bruckner's music as it soars from climax to climax, clad in completely new sound, richly interwoven, unearthly and yet at the same time deliberately and concisely conceived and carried out. This from a man who throughout his whole life continued to speak in his Upper Austrian accent, though his last years were spent in rooms in the Belvedere Palace allotted to him by the Emperor, and who saw himself as nothing but a simple, God-fearing organist who wrote his music for the greater glory of the Almighty.

Not that fame was entirely strange to him, either in Vienna or abroad. In 1871 he had played the organ in London in the Crystal Palace before an audience of seventy thousand, and the audience was so enthralled that, as he later reported, they afterwards carried him about on their shoulders. 'And a lady proposed to me,' he added. 'But she wasn't anything to look at, so I just left her standing!'

Vienna never seems to let her musicians live out their lives. All
of them left behind some unfinished major work. Bruckner was
unable to finish his Ninth Symphony, and in place of the fourth
movement his Te Deum is always played. His Eighth Symphony,
though, was performed during his lifetime with great success,
and Johann Strauss the waltz king, ecstatic about it, was anxious
to make the composer's acquaintance. Bruckner went to see him
and, humble as ever, addressed him as 'Maestro'. But Strauss
refused to accept such a title. 'No, no, you're the Maestro,' he
assured Bruckner. 'I am just a small-time composer from the
suburbs.'

The humility of the one was as ill-founded as that of the other.
Johann Strauss, and before him his father Johann Strauss senior,
wrote music which not merely created a new rage, the waltz, but
was to prove as immortal as many a classic symphony or opera.
Anyone who has heard the Vienna Philharmonics, preferably at
their traditional New Year's Concert, playing Strauss and nothing
but Strauss, will realize what marvellous melodies, what ingenious
rhythms and superb musicianship are contained in these light-
hearted waltzes, galops and polkas.

Church music, as might be expected, is diverse and often
almost flamboyant in Vienna. Plain chant has never made much
headway here, though the Benedictines at the Schotten Monastery
sing it very well. For years in fact a papal dispensation has been
in force which permits other instruments besides the organ to
be played in church. Most visitors head for the Hofburgkapelle
where Masses by Mozart, Haydn and other great classical composers are sung each Sunday by the Vienna Boys' Choir. But
there are other churches where the singing is just as good and
where modern music can also be heard. The Franziskanerkirche
and the Augustinerkirche both have fine choirs and orchestras
and so, of course, has St Stephen's. The Saturday editions of
most Viennese dailies print the 'Church Music' programme for
the following Sunday.

Concerts, too, are advertised in the daily press, but not as much as might be expected. Here again tradition plays an important part. The Viennese concert season, which runs from September till June, consists of an enormous number of concerts, but very many of these are *Abonnements Konzerte*, that is, subscription concerts, organized either by the Gesellschaft der Musikfreunde or the Konzerthausgesellschaft or the Philharmonics. People buy tickets for the whole series, say of orchestral or chamber concerts, and only those left over are sold on the open market. This sounds pretty grim for someone who may only be in Vienna for a short time, but it is not really so bad because, once again, tradition demands that most of these subscription concerts are repeated at least once and often twice. So the same concert can often be heard on three consecutive evenings. Most concerts are, of course, in the evening, but in Vienna the question arises when, say, the Vienna Philharmonics want to give an evening concert, who is to take their place in the Opera, for they are also the State Opera Orchestra. Matinées are the answer, and the Philharmonic concerts have always taken place on Saturday afternoon and Sunday morning. Lights are never turned off during concerts—too many people want to follow the score—so it makes little difference whether the hall is lit by electricity or whether the sun streams in. During the season there may be as many as twenty concerts a week, and tickets for these can be obtained in ticket agencies or at the concert halls themselves.

July and August used to be the dead season. Viennese families try to be in the country then, and in any case during the summer it is really too hot and stuffy in the concert halls, all of them built long before air-conditioning was dreamed of. But the number of tourists who come to Vienna during the summer and want to hear music has increased so greatly that something had to be done about it. During the last few years open-air concerts have been held in the *Arkadenhof*, the main courtyard of the Rathaus, and these have become celebrated. The fare is light and popular—just right for romantic summer evenings. More intimate concerts are held in various palaces throughout the city, where the atmosphere is not so stifling, because windows can be left open and the audience is necessarily limited.

When the Viennese go to the theatre or the opera they usually go to see or hear someone rather than something. It is the actor or the opera singer who is important to them, and what they are playing or singing is often of less account. With concerts it is different. The programme has an important role, and when the Philharmonics tried to play at least one modern work at each of their concerts there was something close to mutiny among their *Stammpublikum*, the 'steadies' who for generations one might almost say have listened to these concerts. In Vienna as elsewhere there is a great dearth of star conductors. Unforgettable *maestri* such as Furtwängler, Clemens Kraus and Bruno Walter are no more and no one seems to have been able to replace them. No one except Herbert von Karajan and he, as everyone knows, left Vienna in a pet and is not likely to return for some time. He certainly had the personality and the musical genius to catch the imagination of the Viennese—and how they loved and hated him at the same time. For the past seven years he had also been director of the Opera and his going has left a painful void. To say, though, that he is irreplaceable is nonsense. Vienna has lost or thrown over many a gifted musician and has still managed to survive. In the meantime such excellent conductors as Karl Böhm, Wolfgang Sawallsich, Joseph Krips and many others are still available to maintain the high level of performances which the Viennese have come to expect.

Salzburg has for so many years been associated with its Festival that it seemed rash to try something similar in Vienna. Even so the *Wiener Festwochen* are slowly but surely becoming part of the city's life, and what they have to offer is magnificent fare. This festival takes place each year from mid May to mid June and has something for everyone: chamber music, orchestral concerts, recitals of all kinds, classical and modern works—one can really pick and choose. The Opera puts on its best performances and so do the theatres. Special exhibitions are held and, added to all this, Vienna is at its best at that time of year—a most attractive lure to visitors.

But it is not only during the tourist season that foreign voices and foreign faces are noticeable in the opera and concert halls. The Academy of Music has for many years been the goal of a great number of students from other countries and particularly from overseas. Its courses for singers and instrumentalists are renowned all over the world, and so it is no longer surprising to see a young Japanese violinist or an equally young American soprano making their début in the city.

Altogether the young people take a very active part in the city's musical life—most concerts have to be repeated especially for the 'Jeunesse Musicale'—and though wireless and television have encroached heavily on music-making in the home, there are still a surprising number of young professional men who find time to play chamber music.

Chapter 4

Music Turned into Stone

AUSTRIAN baroque, in Salzburg or in Vienna, is something very different from the baroque of Italy or even Germany: it is something very personal, something that has developed out of a belated flowering of Gothic architecture followed by a belated unfolding of the Renaissance era. And so by the time other countries were satiated with baroque, and rococo was being evolved, Austria had only reached the point where architects like Johann Bernhard Fischer von Erlach or Lukas von Hildebrandt were building their masterpieces of 'music turned into stone'.

Baroque is not just a style in architecture: it is a state of mind, a mode of life. Gothic man had been succeeded by something very new and different, and modern man was passionately interested in letting everyone around him know that the past was gone for ever, that a new era had begun. So while the Gothic idea embraced eternity and its final end was always God, baroque was something much more earthy; not indeed that it was godless, but its opulent expression of deism was laced with scepticism and cynicism. Gothic man was poor, and for that reason was willing to spend centuries on a building, placing stone upon hewn stone, erecting something stable, mighty and perfect. All that was too slow for modern man. He had money and he wanted to see something for it. He built with brick and mortar, quickly: instead of marble he used stucco, and rich, gilded churches and palaces arose within the span of a single generation.

In Vienna all this can be seen very clearly. St Stephen's took two hundred years to build, and even then was never completed. It was built because a church, and later a cathedral, was needed. The Karlskirche (St Charles's Church), one of Fischer von Erlach's masterpieces, was planned, as were so many baroque churches, not because of any special need for a new church but in thanksgiving for the delivery from the plague at the beginning of the eighteenth century. It took twenty-three years to build. It is a princely church, just as St Stephen's is the people's church. The Emperor Charles VI, who ordered it to be built as his votive church, calculated exactly how much each crownland and each of his dominions must contribute towards its erection. Who reckoned what was to be paid for and by whom when St Stephen's was being built?

Baroque architecture as a whole was the architecture of princes. It imposed itself from above and it was the noble families who furthered it and its architects. There is no doubt that the finest collection of central European baroque is to be found in Austria, and especially in Vienna. Admittedly finer individual examples exist elsewhere, but such fullness, such variety and such a high level of all-round perfection are only to be seen here.

There is, of course, a great difference between baroque and baroque even in Vienna. On the Graben stands the Pestsäule, a Trinity Column which, again, is a votive offering, this time by the Emperor Leopold I as a thanksgiving for the plague having spared at least a proportion of Vienna's population. Leopold can be seen kneeling at the foot of the column, an ugly, bizarre creature with a superb Hapsburg lip, but nevertheless a man of many gifts and a great deal of humanity. The column put up in 1687, which was designed by the leading artists and craftsmen of the day, including the young J. B. Fischer von Erlach, was something entirely new and startling: a mixture of theatrical hyperbole, fervent faith and joyous rapture.

Only a generation later, in 1713, Charles VI, after a further plague epidemic, had another monument built. This is the Josefsäule, the St Joseph's Column, on the Hohe Markt not far away from the Graben. It is just as baroque as the other, but what a world of difference lies between that exuberant almost voluptuous expression of faith and this cool, delicately delineated and exactly formed group beneath its leafy canopy. It was designed by J. B. Fischer von Erlach, and the work was carried out by his son Josef Emmanuel.

Anyone who insists that baroque means nothing to him, that there is simply too much to it, too many writhing figures, too much gilt trumpery, should look at these two columns and then go and look for 'his' baroque, and I refuse to believe that he will not somewhere, here in Vienna, stop and exclaim: 'Why how beautiful!', and be shocked to realize that it is hated, despised baroque.

The greatest exponent of this perfection of style in Vienna is doubtless J. B. Fischer von Erlach. No other architect of his generation was quite his equal, though such masters as von Hildebrandt, who built the Belvedere Palace, the Schwarzenberg Palace and completed the Peterskirche among other things, or Jakob Prandtauer, whose greatest achievement was Melk Monastery on the Danube, come close to rivalling him.

Fischer von Erlach's most famous works in Vienna are typical for the baroque idea: the Karlskirche, symbol of heaven on earth, and the National Library, symbol of modern learning and modern man.

When Charles VI had the Karlskirche built it commanded a view across fallow land and vineyards, since it stood far beyond the city walls, and even today, though the city has encroached on all sides, its green copper dome may still be seen from far and wide. The conception of the church, with its pillared portico and the two towering, free-standing columns on each side, engraved with reliefs depicting scenes from the life of St Charles Borromeo, and topped by the brilliant green dome, is magnificent. The interior, too, with its sweeping light and handsome decorations, fills one with admiration, though it may not appeal to one personally. For myself I have no real feelings of affection for it. What I do love is the Josefsplatz which, with the National Library, is the most perfect square in Vienna and one of the loveliest squares anywhere.

But to savour this beauty completely the National Library must also be seen from inside. The main hall is considered the finest library in the world. The room stretches the entire length of the buildings, and the central hall beneath the dome is divided from the smaller side halls only by groups of pillars. The frescoes are the work of Daniel Gran, one of Austria's greatest baroque painters. In the centre of the hall stands the statue of the Emperor Charles VI, builder of the library, and the walls are lined with shelf upon shelf of beautifully bound volumes and ancient globes. This is indeed perfection, and even Fischer von Erlach was never again to surpass it.

The National Library was built in the years 1723–6 and Daniel Gran added the frescoes in 1730. Shortly before that, in 1722, Hildebrandt had completed his own particular masterpiece, the Belvedere Palace which Prince Eugene of Savoy wanted as his summer residence. His winter palace in the Himmelpfortgasse, which now houses the Ministry of Finance, had been built by Fischer von Erlach with additions by Hildebrandt some years earlier, and with its beautiful staircase it again proves the master's ingenuity and craftsmanship.

The Belvedere consists of two completely separate buildings: the Upper and the Lower Belvedere, between which unfold the gentle slopes of the Belvedere Gardens, divided into symmetrical patterns by paths and staircases and bewitching with their clipped hedges and playing fountains. This is only one of many such 'garden palaces' which the nobility built at that time in the suburbs of the Imperial City. In 1716 Lady Mary Wortley Montagu, after a visit to the garden palace of the Schönborn family, wrote home that she must admit that never had she seen anything more pleasing and charming than the Viennese suburbs, for they were large and filled with beautiful palaces. Most of these palaces are still standing, lovely as ever but, alas, no longer in the suburbs, but right within the modern city. Even so their large gardens—the Liechtenstein gardens in the Ninth District, the Schwarzenberg gardens in the Third and the Auersperg gardens, now attached to a restaurant, in the Eighth, are but a few examples—are still oases of green lawns and spreading trees.

The baroque passion for symmetry in architecture resulted not only in the two Belvedere palaces, providing a perfect vis-à-vis for each other, but also in Schönbrunn Palace and the Gloriette, the royal family's own summer palace, which even today is still standing in one of the outer districts of Vienna. Maria Theresa, whose favourite residence this was, used to ride the considerable distance to the Hofburg in the centre of the city every day.

The original plans for Schönbrunn, which Fischer von Erlach the elder drew up in 1695 for his erstwhile pupil the Emperor Joseph I, had something of an illusionary character and we can still admire its idealistic conception on an engraving of the times. Where today stands the Gloriette on the heights facing the palace, this should itself have stood, to be connected with the lower buildings by innumerable terraces and cascades. The buildings which we know are much more modest, although the original palace erected under Joseph I and Charles VI was added to by Maria Theresa: the garden front by Nicolaus Pacassi shows a marked trend towards rococo, being lighter and more ephemeral than Fischer von Erlach's main front in its imposing strength and nobility.

If St Stephen's is the oldest and dearest symbol of Vienna, then Schönbrunn follows a close second. Although the palace is said to have fifteen hundred rooms, it does not really impress one as being extraordinarily large and extravagant in the way that Versailles or even Blenheim Palace does. Indeed Maria Theresa with her sixteen children had to make very exact calculations to enable everyone to be housed in accordance with Spanish Court etiquette, which required each member of the royal family to have a bedroom, drawing-room, reception-room, ante-chamber and study, even if he were still a baby in arms. This meant that her children were housed here, there and everywhere, in fact anywhere where suitable sets of rooms were to be found, and visitors wishing to pay their respects to all the archdukes and archduchesses could spend a whole day hurrying upstairs and downstairs and along endless corridors, from one wing of the palace to the other, so that they might do everything in the right order, beginning with a visit first to the eldest son.

The showrooms in the palace, which can be visited, and on great state occasions are still in use, are similar to others like them the world over, but the actual living quarters of the Empress, her family and her successors are intimate and delightful. Although two generations have passed since the Emperor Francis Joseph died here, quietly and modestly in his iron truckle bed, the whole palace still breathes life, perhaps because it continues to live on in the affection of the Viennese, who can be seen on Sundays streaming through courtyards and porticos into the palace gardens beyond.

Although Maria Theresa is mainly responsible for Schönbrunn as it is now, there are others whose memories also linger on here.

Her daughter Maria-Antonia spent a happy, giddy childhood at the palace and no shadow of her tragic future as Queen Marie Antoinette of France fell across it. Napoleon resided here and an attempt on his life was made here in 1809. The golden imperial eagles which crown the obelisks flanking the entrance gateway date from those days. His son, the King of Rome, pale and tragic, his blond figure surrounded by an aura of romance, was to die here in 1832. It is only a few years since his remains were taken from Vienna to Paris to rest next to those of his father.

But the palace has happier memories too. It saw the wedding of Joseph II and the birth of Francis Joseph, whose diamond jubilee was also celebrated here. Like Maria Theresa, Francis Joseph spent a great deal of his time in Schönbrunn, particularly in his later years, and the figure of the old Emperor, bowed and grey, promenading slowly each morning in the small Kammergarten, immediately next to the palace, the monarch's private garden, was a familiar sight to all Vienna.

The lovely, spreading park itself had been opened to the public

D

by the Emperor Joseph II, just as he had opened the gardens of his palace in the Augarten and the Prater, those endless reaches of riverside woodland which were his hunting grounds along the Danube. His generosity did not meet with general approval, particularly on the part of the nobility, who grumbled that there was nowhere for them to go any more if they wanted to be amongst themselves. Joseph's typical and sarcastic reply was that if that were the case they had better promenade in the Kapuzinergruft, the Hapsburg burial ground, where they could be certain of being amongst only the greatest in the land.

Maria Theresa herself opened the Schönbrunn Zoo in 1752, but long before that time, in 1552, the Archduke Maximilian, who was later to be the Emperor Maximilian II, on his return from Spain had treated the Viennese population to a display of unprecedented grandeur and surprises. The Viennese of those days, as of these, loved to gape, to see processions and uniforms, flags and anything that was colourful and exotic. That procession was a never-to-be-forgotten spectacle. Behind the Archduke, who drove in a carriage drawn by eight white horses, came courtiers bearing parrots, exotic blooms from the New World, glowing metals and sparkling jewels. There were a troop of monkeys on a leash, a camel, a dromedary and then, finally, as the unforgettable climax, there came an elephant. The Viennese raved and from that moment elephants have been their declared darlings, and are still ruling favourites in the zoo.

The Emperor Max had buildings put up for his outlandish animals, which were added to from time to time and were an object of curiosity for generations of Viennese. Later Prince Eugene of Savoy had a private zoo, and Maria Theresa incorporated this in the royal collection and housed them all in Schönbrunn. Its baroque character, with its delightful octagonal central pavilion, is still easily recognizable, and the word Schönbrunn spoken by any Viennese child means the zoo and nothing else: a visit there is one of the annual pleasures generations of children have regarded as their due.

If the zoo is the children's paradise, then the avenues of clipped chestnuts, the gravel paths and beautifully laid-out flower beds in the gardens are the delight of the elderly. They can walk quietly here, up the meandering zigzag to the Gloriette, a true 'folly' and no mere garden pavilion, which faces the palace and from which on clear summer evenings there is a lovely view of the city to the east. They can visit the Schöne Brunnen, the spring from which the palace takes its name, or can dally in the orangery.

There is something for everybody in Schönbrunn. In the summer months, when most Viennese theatres are closed, one can come here to the most charming of baroque theatres, the little Schönbrunn Schloss Theater, and in surroundings unchanged from the days when Haydn at Maria Theresa's command gave a performance of his opera *Dido* with the Esterházy Court Orchestra, one can listen to similar baroque operas or plays, as delightful to the eye and ear as ever.

Or there is the Wagenburg, a unique collection of coaches and carriages housed in the Empress Elisabeth's former Winter Riding School. It is not spectacular, but history seems to come alive as we look at the imposing coronation coach of the Emperor Charles VI, which is 250 years old and is said to be the most beautiful carriage in the world; or at that other coronation coach, so different in style and atmosphere—the coach Napoleon used when he had himself crowned King of Lombardy. Glancing out into the park one may imagine his son, the little King of Rome, driving about in his white-and-gold children's carriage, pulled by white merino sheep.

Returning from Schönbrunn to the centre of the town seems at first like coming to another world. But when we look around, how familiar the other baroque palaces and churches, the town houses and monuments now appear. Not all of them may appeal, they may lack that feeling of simultaneous grandeur and simplicity, but still we shall know what to look for. And we shall find it everywhere in Vienna—along narrow streets around St Stephen's, like the Singerstrasse, on squares like Am Hof or the Freyung, farther out beyond the Ringstrasse among gardens—we shall find it and enjoy it, because it is an essential part of the town and without it much of the joyous sparkle which has seldom failed to bewitch its visitors would be gone.

Chapter 5

City of Paintings

WHILE music and architecture have always seemed at home in Austria, painting has never flourished. Its two dimensions seemed too limited for local talent and appropriately enough its first real flowering was in baroque times when painters endeavoured to thrust further into a third dimension, and illusionary and colourful allegories burst out and spread across ceilings in attempts to encompass the heavens themselves. But the artists working in Vienna were initially imported from Italy; for baroque painting, itself only a small part of the grand perfection constituting the baroque idea of universality, was international rather than local. 'The Glorification of Prince Eugene of Savoy' in the marble hall of the Lower Belvedere, for instance, is by Martin Altomonte, and his contemporaries seemed to rejoice in the same sort of exactly calculated turmoil of colour and form: only Daniel Gran perhaps created a serener, almost classical style.

If there had been no baroque architecture with stucco ceilings crying out for ornamentation, painting would have played only a minor role in Austria and Vienna. The only artist of that time whose genius compares with Fischer von Erlach's and is of European stature is a sculptor, Raphael Donner. He is not a true baroque artist—he was born in 1692 and his works lack much of the passion, the upswept heroic movement which characterizes baroque art. Instead his figures, mostly cast in shimmering, softly subtle lead, are relaxed: they are imbued with gentleness and an air of melancholy, not on any account to be mistaken for weakness.

His greatest work is the fountain on the Neue Markt square, in which each of the four figures gathered around a marble basin represents an Austrian river. Providence is seated in the centre. These bronze figures are copies of the original ones in lead, which date from 1739 and are in the museum in the Lower Belvedere. They should be seen if possible because the copies lack much of their finesse.

Austria, and particularly Vienna, although it led the world in music for so long, has always stood outside the great art movements. Nothing like a Viennese school or movement appears until the nineteenth and twentieth centuries. Strangely it was when the rest of European art was going through a period of stagnation and seemed to be wavering between the old and the new that Viennese art flashed on to the scene.

'Flashed' is perhaps an inappropriate word in connection with Biedermeier art, that gentle, romantic, homely expression of everything which now seems to us to be overflowing with sentimentality and pathos. Yet it was the Biedermeier era in the nineteenth century which produced some of Vienna's finest painters.

The Österreichische Museum is housed in the Upper Belvedere, and for me there is always the temptation of looking out of the window at the Belvedere Gardens and the spreading carpet and skyline of the city beyond rather than at the paintings—but perhaps it is the turning from one to the other which best enables us to appreciate both of them.

Biedermeier and 'old Vienna' are closely related to early Victorian England. In the *genre* paintings there is that same feeling for realism, meticulous detail glossed over with sentiment; while the portraits of the Viennese masters of the time recall Sir Thomas Lawrence. Yet this post-revolutionary painting, these pictures of family life, of sun-drenched landscapes and unimportant details, fitted perfectly into the Vienna of the period, much of which has remained unchanged.

Few examples of Biedermeier domestic architecture are left in the centre of the city, which in the latter half of the nineteenth century, during the so-called Gründerperiode when the city walls finally fell and the Ringstrasse was planned and executed, was

enriched with handsome patrician houses. The artistic and archi-
tectural expression of that era, a conglomeration of many styles,
from ancient Greek and Roman to Gothic and Renaissance, which
became the glory and curse of the spacious Ringstrasse, now
seems the height of bad taste to us. But out beyond the Ring and
the Gürtel, that second 'belt' as its name tells us, which divided
the inner suburbs from the actual country villages at the foot of
the Vienna Woods, many small, comfortable, bourgeois houses
still exist. Their square windows are still hidden behind white
net curtains, and their courtyards, tucked away from the outer
world, have creeping vines, green painted wooden galleries and
stairs and possibly an old creaking well. The spirit which inspires
these houses can be sensed even today: Napoleon was gone for
ever, the Vienna Congress had danced itself into history, this was
the time for convalescence, for *Gemütlichkeit*.

One painter of that time stands out from all the others, not
only because in the Österreichische Museum there is a very large
collection of his works, but because he developed into something
greater than the brilliant portrait painter and delightful *genre*
specialist he started out to be. This is Waldmüller, and what he is
most admired for today is the sunlight which floods his later
landscapes, such as his paintings of the Vienna Woods and the
Prater. In the end Waldmüller left Biedermeier painting far
behind and pushed forward into the field of impressionism.

As might be expected, the paintings which accompanied the
Ringstrasse fashion in architecture were superficial, boisterous
and overladen. This was the time when Makart reigned supreme,
not only with his showy portraits and luscious, larger-than-life
nudes, but also with his style of interior decoration which featured
velvet trappings, silk tassels and dimness combined with rustic
benches and negligent arrangements of lightly swaying reeds
and Japanese fans. The procession which he arranged at the time
of the silver wedding of Emperor Francis Joseph and Empress
Elisabeth in 1879, along the newly opened Ringstrasse, was the
sort of splendid spectacle on the verge of dreamland that the

Viennese love. Makart himself took part in it, dressed in Rubens-
esque garments and riding a white horse, and the citizens
applauded him more than they did the royal couple themselves.

The Ringstrasse itself is not simply a monstrous collection of
overblown buildings as people nowadays are inclined to regard
it. Admittedly we smile as we pass the Opera (neo-Renaissance),
the Parliament (neo-Classical), the Rathaus (neo-Gothic), and so
on. Considering the possibilities it could have been so much
worse. The 'Ring' is one of the most beautiful boulevards in the
world, for the unity of its conception is difficult to match.

Even if we can think of nothing else in favour of this period,
then we should at least be grateful for the Heldenplatz, with the
two really fine equestrian statues of the Archduke Charles and
Prince Eugene of Savoy. The view across bunched lilacs and
clipped rows of red chestnuts towards a backdrop of buildings
old and new is enchanting.

Just as the modest, diminutive art forms of Biedermeier times
had been replaced by the large-scale, overpowering Ringstrassen
forms, so now another turn of the wheel brought the revolutionary *fin-de-siècle* painters of the *Jugendstil*, a movement akin to *Art
Nouveau*. The Zentralsparkasse on the Kochplatz, with its black
pinhead ornamentation, belongs to this period, when Otto
Wagner was designing buildings that were bare and shockingly
functional—admired in theory, perhaps, but considered too
revolutionary in practice. The Zentralsparkasse now seems
dreary rather than revolutionary.

In painting the new art was represented by Gustav Klimt. He
started conservatively—some of the frescoes for the staircases
in the Burgtheater are his—and won the approval of the Emperor
Francis Joseph himself. Then he took part in a competition for the
murals for the new university and there was a storm of protest
against his languid and purely ornamental figures. No one knew
what they represented and his designs were not accepted. His very
individualistic style, however, continued to develop. His portraits,
mostly of beautiful women, consisted of gold and silver ornaments,

often the face alone retaining its human likeness. His landscapes
were two-dimensional coloured squares which bewitch the eye.

A feeling of unease, of introvert anxiety that was abroad even
before the First World War, is apparent in the works of the
painter Romako, a contemporary of Makart, whose paintings
were laced with a strange eeriness beneath their brilliant surface,
but it finds its most remarkable expression in the startling drawings and paintings of Egon Schiele.

Paintings by Klimt, Romako, Schiele and Makart can be seen
both in the Österreichisches Museum in the Upper Belvedere
and in the Museum des XX Jahrhunderts in the Schweizer
Garten next to the Südbahnhof (South station).

Schiele's work is perhaps most closely related to Munch's; it
too is bizarre and anxiety laden. His technique is masterly and his
message often overpowering. His own boyish, birdlike face and
narrow starved body appear again and again in his paintings,
and there is a breathtaking mixture of brutality and gentleness
in his work, whether in one of his large canvases at the Österreichisches Museum or in the charcoal drawings of a baby in the
Albertina. He died in 1918 at the age of twenty-eight during the
flu epidemic, and once again Vienna lost one of its brilliant sons
before he had been able to fulfil his enormous promise.

Agreed that Vienna is not really a city of painters, it is nevertheless a city of paintings. Whatever one may say against the
Hapsburg dynasty, they were always great art collectors, and in
the Kunsthistorisches Museum Vienna can boast some of the
greatest paintings in the world, including the finest collection of
Breughels, as well as that perfect series of portraits of Spanish
Infantas and Infantes by Velasquez.

The second Hapsburg collection in Vienna is the Albertina,
in the Hofburg, a collection of drawings and works of graphic
art founded by Maria Theresa's favourite son-in-law, Prince
Albert of Sachsen-Teschen. This unique collection includes 140
works by Dürer, among them such old favourites as 'The Hare',
and again it is the personal note behind the collection, the feeling

that someone painstakingly and lovingly gathered it all together, which gives it special appeal.

Before the war there were still a number of private art galleries which could also boast some very fine collections. Now most of them have disappeared, and it is only lately that the Harrach Gallery at least has been reopened. The Harrach Palais on the Freyung, the work of Lukas von Hildebrandt, was badly damaged during the war, the only compensation being that it was restored according to Hildebrandt's original designs and without the foibles added by later generations. The collection consists mainly of Italian, Spanish and Dutch works of the seventeenth century, the period when three members of the Harrach family were enthusiastic collectors.

So even though Vienna is not the birthplace of great painting, it is the home of some of the world's finest pictures.

Chapter 6

'Ein Theater'

ON MILD summer evenings queues can be seen forming outside a very modest wooden ticket office in one of the side streets in Ottakring, Vienna's most populous and at the same time perhaps most volatile district. When you have paid for your ticket you walk into a small open-air theatre and settle down on a hard wooden bench to watch a comedy, tragedy or perhaps a hair-raising thriller. The audience is a responsive one and the acting is so good that everybody is carried away. But it is not only the excellent acting that makes people from all over Vienna trek to this rather shabby little establishment; the great attraction is that it is all entirely unscripted, hence the theatre's name of Tschauners Stegreifbühne (speaking 'off the stirrup' or impromptu). An hour before the curtain rises none of the actors knows what he is to play. The cast are given a short synopsis of the plot, told what parts they are to play and off they go. Every night there is a different play and I have never seen any sign of hesitation from any member of the cast. It is fascinating to watch, and the sort of performance which seems to me the very essence of the theatre. This is the last theatre of its kind to survive, not only in Vienna but in central Europe.

That it should have survived in Vienna is not really surprising. Here the play has always been the thing, and to the Viennese the word 'theatre' does not merely mean play-acting but covers anything exciting, anything perturbing or pleasurable—all is *ein Theater*. The screaming child is told off for making *ein Theater*, the crowd gathered at the street corner to see the goings on after the motor-car rammed the tram are making *ein Theater*, and at the wedding breakfast everything seems to be *ein Theater* too.

Every Viennese baby appears to be born with a sense of drama, and by the time he is grown up he has learnt a great deal about self-dramatization. He loves to feel himself transported into another world and to worship at the shrine of an actor or singer whom he himself may at times knowledgeably criticize; but beware if you attempt to do the same. Everybody goes to the theatre and, if at all possible, to the Burgtheater or Opera. A tram conductor may be just as much an expert on Mozart or Strauss operas as a university professor; an old-age pensioner may be found deep in argument with a teenager about the merits of the latest Grillparzer production as they patiently queue for their standing-room tickets.

It is in fact no mere chance that the Burgtheater, or, as it used to be called, the K. u. K. Hoftheater, i.e. the Imperial and Royal Court Theatre, should be the leading German-speaking theatre anywhere. Here again it is the Hapsburgs, just as stage-struck as their subjects, whom we have to thank for the fact that theatre and opera have always been considered not a luxury but a necessity, so that both Opera and Burgtheater—not to mention the Vienna Philharmonics—have been State-supported for a very long time. Even the Emperor Francis Joseph, who was almost entirely devoid of artistic feeling, loved the theatre and took the greatest personal interest in the Hoftheater and its actors and actresses long before one of them, Katharina Schratt, became his lifelong friend. It is characteristic of Vienna and the position its actors and actresses hold that this friendship with a very fine actress, who was also a self-effacing and understanding woman, had the approval not only of the Empress Elisabeth but of the entire Viennese population.

Perhaps it is because they know that it is their own money which goes into the Burgtheater and Opera that makes the Viennese take such a personal interest in them. Any crises in the management—and they have always abounded, because the fact that an actor is paid a salary like a civil servant does not turn him into one—any queries about casting a particular actor or the possibly

prejudicial treatment of some favourite are discussed as heatedly
as the latest political upheaval, and make as many headlines. An
actor or singer who is lucky enough to hear himself referred to
as 'der' Meyer or 'die' Schuster knows that he has reached the
top, for once his Christian name seems superfluous his fame is
assured.

Not surprisingly it is the dramatists who are Austria's greatest
poets—Grillparzer, Hofmannsthal, Schnitzler, Wildgans. Raimund and Nestroy, those writers of undying visionary allegories
and comedies of biting sarcastic humour, are an integral part of
Vienna.

Franz Grillparzer is perhaps the only great classical dramatist
that Vienna has produced. The fact that he is little known outside
Austria and Germany may be because his dramas—historical
works, mythological tragedies and comedies—are, despite their
lovely, timeless poetry and dramatic values, so closely entwined
with Vienna that only here can they be truly appreciated. The
same can be said of both Raimund and Nestroy, whose comedies
are written mostly in the vernacular, so that a friend of mine from
Germany admitted that she 'just didn't know what they were
talking about'. The problems of translation in these cases are
almost insurmountable.

But the Viennese *patois*, *Wienerisch*, is something more than the
local slang to be found anywhere. Just as everyone goes to the
theatre here, so everyone talks *Wienerisch*. There are, of course,
different degrees and even strong local differences between one
part of the town and another. At Court French or *Wienerisch* was
spoken; any other language, including *Hochdeutsch* (pure German)
stamped the user as a foreigner. The Empress Maria Theresa or
the Emperor Francis Joseph used the same homely expressions
as their liveried servants. Today a university professor talking
to the plumber come to mend his sink will automatically fall into
the familiar Viennese idiom; the actor who has just been declaim-
ing with the purest enunciation on the stage will greet his friends
in the accents of a barrow boy.

Perhaps this is why the Viennese are not so class-conscious as the English; in this they are closer to the Americans. The varieties and nuances of *Wienerisch* are endless and to an expert proclaim the district of Vienna to which the speaker belongs, but there is little division into U and non-U. The state secondary schools are attended by children from the upper middle class right down to the working class, not for lack of other schools but because they are known to be good and no stigma is attached to being educated at one. Admittedly the language the boys use there makes my hair stand on end at times, but as soon as they emerge into their own world they become their normal selves again and use their own, normal language.

All this can be sensed in Viennese drama and poetry, and to hear a German actor, attached to the Burgtheater, struggling manfully to get just the right intonation, the right inflection for the brilliant dialogue of a Hofmannsthal or Schnitzler play makes one writhe with anguish for him. None would dare attempt a Raimund or Nestroy comedy unless he had spent the better part of his life in Vienna.

The present Burgtheater, like the State Opera, was, as far as the auditorium and the stage were concerned, completely rebuilt after the last war, when both were very badly damaged by bombs. The present interior is not very heart-warming, though it is of course large and impressive and the acoustics are excellent. It is possible, however, to get the feeling that the theatre consists almost entirely of magnificent staircases until the acting makes one forget that in externals at least the 'Burg' cannot compete with the other major theatre in Vienna, the Theater in der Josef- stadt, still one of the most perfect baroque theatres in the world. Just to sit there among the red damask boxes and gilt woodwork and to see the many-flamed chandelier slowly rise and dim as the curtain goes up fills one with an expectant glow. Neither are the performances in the Josefstadt, as the theatre is familiarly known, likely to extinguish it.

It may surprise the visitor that almost all the theatres in Vienna are repertory. During a season, which runs from September to the end of June, as many as ten to fifteen plays may be added to a single theatre's repertoire, and one only knows what's on by looking in the newspapers or at the posters which give the programme for the current fortnight. This means of course that it is impossible to book far ahead, and often there is a scramble for opera or theatre tickets when something or someone special is playing.

Even in Vienna there are long runs at times, but on the whole the hankering for something ever changing keeps the repertory system alive. Some of the stars at the Burgtheater may be attached to this institution for a lifetime so that, like that wonderful trage-dienne Hedwig Bleibtreu, who died in 1958, they may celebrate their diamond jubilee as one of its members. They are remembered in hundreds of roles and those lucky enough to have season tickets can, year after year, watch the development and flowering of a favourite actor or actress until the unmistakable glow of starlight surrounds them.

Chapter 7

Typically Viennese

RECENTLY I had to go to the Messepalast, the former Imperial Stables, where nowadays the annual spring and autumn trade fairs are held. The handsome baroque building lies just beyond the Kunsthistorisches Museum and the Naturhistorisches Museum on the Burgring and consists of many wings surrounding many different courtyards. I had been there before, but I got lost all the same and suddenly I found myself in another world.

I walked through a narrow passage, and up some steps, and there I was in what the Viennese call a *Beisl*, a small modest pub, completely cut off from the outside world, set among old trees on what must have been part of the original fortifications. It was lunch time, the place was full and the head waiter, the *Herr Ober*, appeared to know all his guests personally—most of them seemed to be judges and lawyers from the nearby Ministry of Justice, so that the air was filled with titles such as *Herr Oberlandesgerichtsrat*, *Herr Richter* or just plain *Herr Doktor*. No one took the slightest notice of me, except of course the waiter, who was both punctilious and friendly, and I marvelled once again at what out-of-the-way oases of peace can still be found in a city numbering close on two million.

That is of course typically Viennese. There are any number of such secret worlds in Vienna open only to the initiated, and anyone who wants to find them must look for them. There are all sorts of pubs and gardens, churches and coffee-houses, all of them seemingly leading their own separate existence.

Coffee-houses as such seem, alas, to be dying out—their great era is gone for ever. At the beginning of the century the coffee-house you frequented was a clear indication of your profession

THE MAIN HALL OF THE NATIONALBIBLIOTHEK, 'the finest library hall in the whole world' (*page 39*)

DONNER'S GREATEST WORK, the bronze fountain on the Neue Markt

TSCHAUNER'S IMPROMPTU THEATRE is the last of its kind in Central Europe (*page 51*)

THE OLD GALLERIED *Biedermeier* HOUSES in their courtyards are tucked
away from the outer world (*pages 46–7*)

THE VIENNESE POSTMAN has a genius for getting letters to their
destination . . . no problem seems to be too difficult (*page 60*)

THE SCHOTTENKIRCHE on the
Freyung in the background,
a display of *Lederhosen,* and
a citizen who is not
necessarily carrying documents
in his briefcase (*page 61*)

THE CLASSIC
SCHRAMMEL QUARTET
(*below*) is to be found in most
of the *Nobel-Heurigen,*
entertaining the
wine-tasting patrons (*page 63–4*)

AT WHITSUN the streets
are suddenly flooded with
horse-drawn carriages,
decorated with canopies of
artificial flowers (*page 65–6*)

A CARVING OF THE BASILISK
on the front of a house in
the Schönlaterngasse
commemorates a local
legend (*page 72*)

'LINES OF YOUNG GIRLS, all in white, with their black-garbed, white-tied partners' (*page 67*) at the opening of the Opera Ball

AN EXQUISITE PERFORMANCE in an exquisite setting. Members of the Spanish Riding School dancing an intricate figure

A FINE NEW SUBWAY, once fought against, now a source of pride

THE ENORMOUS STADTHALLE, sports arena, concert hall, conference centre

or your inclinations. It was very much a club world, a home from home, where you could spend all day immersed in your studies or the newspapers of half the world over a single cup of coffee and innumerable glasses of cold, clear water, which the waiter automatically replaced as soon as he thought that some of its freshness was lost. You could also take part in discussions or play a meditative game of chess or possibly draughts or cast a partisan eye over the shoulder of a *Tarock* player.

The first coffee-house had been opened after the second Turkish siege in 1683 by Georg Franz Kolschitzky. He had acted as an Austrian spy and so knew that a delicate, aromatic brew could be made from the insignificant green beans, many bags of which the Turks had left behind. The Viennese took to coffee-drinking very quickly, for by 1730 there were as many as forty-five coffee-houses scattered throughout the town. They were usually small and intimate; it was only in the latter half of the nineteenth century that palatial establishments, filled with plush and mirrors, in-numerable marble-topped tables and glittering chandeliers, silver salvers and lace doilies, came into being. Today these in their turn are disappearing for lack of custom and lack of staff. What still exist are espresso bars—where strong black coffee drips continually from steaming machines and customers are gone as quickly as they came—and the smaller, shabby coffee-houses, where you feel at home and relaxed, where the *Herr Ober* knows you and your wishes and you have at least a nodding acquaintance with the dark gentleman at table No. 3 and the pale student over in the corner.

What also remain are the innumerable sorts of coffee you can order, requiring a veritable coffee lexicon to interpret the list to the stranger. You can order *Kappuziner* (a small cup of black coffee) which also goes by the name of *Mocca* or *Kleiner Schwarzer* and may possibly be *gestreckt* or *kurz*, in accordance with the exact potency desired. The women customers may prefer a *Kleiner Brauner* (black coffee with a dash of milk), a *Melange* (large cup of coffee and milk in equal parts), a *Schale Gold* (more milk than coffee) or the traditional *Einspänner* (black coffee served in a glass

E

and topped with whipped cream, which invariably spills down the side of the glass as you try to add powdered sugar). The glasses of water continue to accompany each cup of coffee, for the Viennese are inordinately and rightly proud of their drinking water, which for the past century has come to them direct from the mountains round the Schneeberg and still retains most of its Alpine freshness and flavour.

The days when you knew exactly in which coffee-house a particular person or profession was to be found are gone. There may, however, still be a note of familiarity between the *Herr Ober* and his regular guests. To the latter traditionally belongs that comic, simple and lovable character 'Graf Bobby', who for many years has enlivened Viennese wit with his comments and adventures, so that he has become almost a person of flesh and blood and not merely a legendary figure of fun. There are innumerable stories about him and some of the jokes are almost existentialist in their absurdity. Sometimes though they are very telling and characterize not only Graf Bobby but the Vienna he lives in. One of my favourite stories about him is the following:

Graf Bobby goes to his regular café, sits down and beckons to the *Herr Ober*.

'Please bring me a cup of coffee and the *Völkische Beobachter*' (a notorious Nazi newspaper).

'Herr Graf,' says the waiter, 'I can bring you the coffee but not the *Völkische Beobachter*—it doesn't exist any more.'

'All right,' says Graf Bobby, 'just bring me the coffee.'

A little later he calls the junior waiter.

'Piccolo, please bring me a glass of *Sliwowitz* and the *Völkische Beobachter*.'

'Herr Graf,' says the junior waiter, 'I'll bring you the *Sliwowitz* straight away, but the *Völkische Beobachter* you can't have.'

'All right,' says Graf Bobby, 'just bring me the *Sliwowitz*.'

A little later he calls the *Herr Ober* again.

'Could I have a glass of water and the *Völkische Beobachter*?'

The *Herr Ober* gets a little annoyed. 'Herr Graf,' he says, 'I've already told you, the *Völkische Beobachter* doesn't exist any longer, those times are gone, we've got rid of the Nazi swine—haven't you realized that yet?'

'Oh, I have,' says Graf Bobby; 'it's just that I so much enjoy hearing about it.'

Nowadays, one feels, Graf Bobby would not be very happy in many of the coffee-houses, where there are more women than men and bridge has replaced *Tarock*, but he might well end up by visiting the Café Hawelka in the Dorotheergasse, which is one of the few to retain a really personal note.

The place itself is rather dingy, but you can meet almost anybody there from leading poets and painters to bearded students and their ' Juliette Greco' girl friends. There too you can discuss anything with anybody, and since there is never space enough for everyone to have a table of his own, you are likely to be formally introduced to your neighbour by the proprietor, so that conversation need never lag.

If the Café Hawelka is typical of what remains of coffee-house society, then Demel's reigns supreme among the more feminine places of relaxation, the *Conditorei*, the pastry shop.

Most of these establishments, and there are very many, have moved with the times and have modern furniture and modern equipment. Pretty waitresses catch your eye as much as the delicacies displayed in streamlined refrigerators. Not so Demel's on the Kohlmarkt. There nothing has changed an iota for at least fifty years. The rooms are small, the upright chairs and tiny marble-topped tables anything but comfortable. There is a Smoking Salon, which means that smoking in the other rooms is not looked upon kindly. If a new, younger waitress is engaged it's the talk of the town, because the black-frocked and white-aproned matrons who wend their stately way from the back of the premises to their tables are as much part of Demel's as the mahogany-tiered sideboards from which you choose savouries or sweets, or the table at the back spread with biscuits and wafers, cakes and pastries, which may not have that modern, smooth look but which do, literally, melt in your mouth. Altogether it is a leisurely place and to appreciate it you must not be in a rush, otherwise its slow-motion rhythm may enervate rather than soothe.

So far 'typically Viennese' has largely meant institutions and places, but of course there are also typical Viennese characters. No one quite so obviously 'typical' as the London 'bobby' or the American train guard can be found here, but let me sing a hymn of praise to an often forgotten, often unnoticed, figure in Vienna's daily life—the postman.

The uniform is traditional—one of the few that have remained so, now that the policeman's familiar dark green, lengthy over-coats and shiny leather belts have been replaced by more modern versions reaching just below the knees—of dark blue serge, piped with yellow, the postal emblem decorating perky but comfortable caps. What is so special, so typical about the Viennese postman is his genius for getting letters to their destination and his personal interest and ambition that they should do so. No problem seems to be too difficult; the postal authorities and the postmen seem to take real pleasure in fitting together puzzles, in discovering just whom some particular missive might be for. When I tell my postman I think he's wonderful—having just received a letter addressed to me by name but at quite a different address, he shrugs—nothing special about that. That a letter addressed to an American friend who had just arrived in Vienna reached him—at no extra charge—although merely addressed to 'Sparks, Vienna, Konradsheimstrasse', whereas the actual address should have been, 'Sparks, c/o Konradsheim, Prater-strasse 21, Vienna II', seems close to miraculous.

The Viennese love eating, no good denying it, and doubtless most of them eat too much. Many people on first arriving are surprised to see almost everyone going around carrying an attaché case. Children use them as school satchels and lawyers actually do keep their briefs in them, but then you see a policeman carry-ing one, and the bricklayer or the chimney-sweep, the tram

conductor going off duty or the clerk on his way home; all seem
to be inseparable from their brown leather cases—some of which
have reached an advanced stage of disrepair. After a time you
discover that what emerges from them is not heavy tomes or files
but bottles of beer, rolls filled with sausage, perhaps an apple, a
cheese sandwich to keep the wolf from the door during the
afternoon, or even a small pannikin in which to warm up some
goulash when the occasion arises.

This gift for endless eating has always filled me with awe. Dis-
posing of the contents of the attaché cases during working hours
is not as time-wasting as might be imagined, for the Viennese
mostly eat and work at the same time—in the post office you'll
get your letter stamped while in an open drawer lies a half-eaten
Wurstsemmel; at the police station your inquiry will be answered
promptly while one of the policeman's hands is deftly and
apparently automatically unwrapping some greaseproof paper
from a thick chunk of bread and lard; and the carpenter can give
his instructions to his mates just as easily with his mouth full of
liver sausage and with a bottle of beer to emphasize his points.

It all helps to create a relaxed atmosphere. Inhibitions and
complexes are swallowed up in a sea of food and drink, but if this
day-to-day feasting does not always do the trick then the Viennese
have another, super, outlet—the *Heuriger*.

Wine and Vienna have been associated with each other not
merely for a couple of hundred years, like coffee, but since Roman
times. It was the Emperor Probus who suggested the planting of
vines on the hills surrounding Vienna. The Roman garrison was
at first not greatly taken with the sour wine which was the result
but later changed its mind, and as time went on the continued
tipsiness of the soldiery began to cause scandal. Seeking a remedy,
the Legate Gallienus discovered that when nuts were eaten with
the wine it was less potent. So nut trees were planted wherever
possible and they flourished, particularly in today's Nineteenth
District. There are still Nussdorf, the Nussberg and the
Nusswaldgasse as reminders of them.

From that time onward Vienna without its wine was unthink-
able. True, the vineyards remained outside the precincts of the
city for many centuries, but the vintners and husbandmen played
an important role in its life, and the question 'What sort of wine
will it be this year?' continues to be of major importance. The size
of the harvest and the sweetness of the wine vary enormously,
though nowadays wine is never so sour as in the days of the
Emperor Frederick III. He ordered a certain vintage to be taken
to St Stephen's graveyard so that the mortar used for the cathedral
spire, then under construction, might be mixed with it.

About half the vines grown in Vienna are in the Nineteenth
District, in Döbling, and it is there that most of the *Heurigen*
taverns are to be found. The idea of drinking *Heuriger*, the new
vintage, goes back to the late eighteenth century, but it did not
really become popular until Biedermeier times when the discovery
of nature and a certain romanticism drove the people out of the
town to seek their pleasure in the surrounding countryside.
Visits to the vintners to sample the new wine were a matter of
grave importance and a private rather than a public pleasure.
Even today it is the smaller places in Grinzing, Sievering or Nussdorf which still boast a clientèle of connoisseurs, while the more
flashy, populous establishments, which do not necessarily sell
merely their own or merely new wine, cater for the general public
and tourists.

Each vintner is allotted two or three weeks during the year
when he may sell his wine on his own premises. He ties a bunch
of pine branches to a pole and hangs it outside his house like a flag
to attract the passer by. At the same time his regular customers
receive neatly printed invitations stating that the vintner takes
pleasure in announcing that he will be selling his wine during
the coming weeks. His house usually has only one or two windows
facing the street, while the main front runs along a narrow cobbled
courtyard leading towards the press house where the wine press
stands. If it is winter a room is emptied of its usual furniture and
wooden tables and benches are put up. In the summer the same

tables and benches are put into the courtyard or stand at the back of the house beneath a few trees or in the vineyard itself. The wine is served in big jugs, its colour pale yellow, golden or tinged with green according to the sort of grape used. The vintner's wife may sit at a separate table and sell bread and ham, eggs and bacon and the dry, hard ginger biscuits known as *Weinbeisser*. Mostly, though, people arrive carrying parcels of food which they spread out before them, and while the atmosphere becomes mellower with every glass of wine drunk, great chunks of black bread and ham are carved expertly to go with it. When it gets dark fairy lights strung from one tree to the next are lighted, sometimes there are candles or lanterns, a man with a guitar appears and strums away, flower-sellers and beggars pass from table to table, and while lovers become silent and draw close to each other perfect strangers get into intimate conversation. If the director of a factory discovers that he has been discussing life with one of his lowliest workers no loss of face is involved—the *Heuriger* makes us all equal and equally befuddled if we have had just that extra glass which proves our undoing. Viennese wine appears to be very light, and when its potency is realized it is too late—so beware!

At first the wine may seem a little sour, particularly the *Heuriger*, though of course it depends largely on the sort and vintage you are drinking. Lately, however, the popularity of Viennese wines has grown prodigiously and can easily compete with the Rieslings and Green Veltliner of the Rhine and Moselle valleys. While the vines grown round Vienna itself and farther afield in the Wachau valley produce wine mostly of the light, effervescent type, that from vines grown to the south of Vienna, around Gumpolds-kirchen and Baden and in the Burgenland, is heavier and sweeter.

The music which goes with wine-drinking is also typically Viennese. The ditties are sweet and lilting, humorously senti-mental and easy on the ear. They have remained unchanged for the last hundred years and the classic Schrammel Quartet, con-sisting of two violins, guitars and accordion, which is called after the Schrammel brothers who first played in this combination, is to be found in most of the *Nobel-Heurigen* which cater for an international public. They can play anything by ear, whether it is the latest jazz hit or something our grandmothers used to hum. There is too in Grinzing a *Heuriger* where the owner himself sings —folk-songs from his native Styria and old settings of tunes familiar from childhood. There is something strangely moving in listening to this burly man, shirt sleeves pushed back beyond his elbows, green apron tied around his massive waist, singing with the sweet child-like tones of a counter-tenor, while the moon rises slowly above the vine-clad hills and only the shadows and silhouettes of those around us, and the gently clinking glasses, remind us that we are not alone.

The Viennese love entertainment of any sort, and just as they will happily relax at a *Heuriger* over a glass of wine or go to the theatre to participate in its strange mixture of reality and make-believe, so too they will go to church expecting not merely religious ceremonies but also a certain amount of entertainment. This is because their religious sentiments and beliefs are based less on theological articles of faith than on their own personal feelings and the traditions which have made religion part of their everyday existence.

Vienna is, of course, almost entirely Catholic: the Reformation was never able to make itself permanently felt here and only a sprinkling of Protestant churches, mostly Lutheran, remain. The cool formality of the Protestant faith makes little response to the Viennese desire for richness and extravagance in Church matters. Though the Viennese may obey the laws of the Church only according to their own interpretation of them, religion is so very much part of the people that it is an essential feature of their character and language. This is why St Stephen's Cathedral was rebuilt laboriously, and at the cost of real sacrifice on the part of much of the population, long before even a small percentage of human habitations had been reconstructed.

How well I remember the day when the restored *Pummering* returned to Vienna. The huge bell, originally cast from Turkish guns, had crashed through the vaulting of the cathedral and had been smashed on the floor when the church was in flames. Later it was recast from the same material and brought back to Vienna from the foundry in Upper Austria. It might have been a royal procession. There were crowds everywhere along the streets as the bell, crowned with flowers and ribbons, was borne along to its final destination, the north tower of St Stephen's.

Viennese Catholics may be somewhat lax about attending Mass each Sunday—if they want to get out into the country they are sure God won't take it amiss and they have no feelings of guilt about it—but there are moments when they flock to church. Not only the Midnight Mass at Christmas but the Holy Week ceremonies play an important part in their lives. These ceremonies are again an odd mixture of liturgy and popular custom, thousands of people trudging from church to church to visit the 'Holy Graves', altars which, beautifully decked with flowers, have been fashioned into something akin to a grave built into a rock in which the figure of the dead Saviour may be seen reposing. Some of these 'Holy Graves' have been in use for generations and the statues and trappings that go with them are very lovely.

In the autumn too there comes a day, the 1st November, All Saints, when the town is alive with people from all over the place. This time it is not the churches they are making for but the cemeteries, and by evening there are few graves without candles flickering in their lanterns or a wreath or bunch of flowers placed on them. These visits to the cemeteries, particularly the Zentralfriedhof, are almost a cult, and transport services carry more passengers on that day than on any other throughout the year. The Zentralfriedhof is worth visiting not only because of its immense size, or because the graves of most of Vienna's great sons and daughters are here, but because this vast spreading park is the home of rare birds of many sorts, and on a quiet afternoon the nightingale can be heard.

The almost childlike interpretation of religion is perhaps most evident around Whitsun when the streets of the First District are suddenly flooded with horse-drawn carriages, decorated with the most astonishing canopies of artificial flowers. In these monstrous bowers of yellow, pink or pale lilac feathers or plastic blooms sit girls in pastel-coloured party frocks and boys in dark blue serge, most of them clutching not only a prayer book but also the string attached to an extra large balloon emblazoned with 'St Stephen's' or perhaps the words *Zur Heiligen Firmung*, while opposite them sit elderly couples dressed in their best clothes, with benign, beaming expressions. This is the time when boys and girls are confirmed, and since only a bishop can confer this sacrament thousands of children crowd into St Stephen's for the occasion. But the sacred aspects have long been submerged by the popular customs attached to it, which consist not only in the decorated carriages and cars but also in the presentation of a watch and an afternoon spent either in the Wurstelprater or at a big tea on the Kahlenberg, or both. The atmosphere in the streets around St Stephen's is flavoured at that time with the almost forgotten scent of horses, and their neighing and pawing mingle incongruously with the noise of motor traffic.

Vienna is famous the world over for its lovely melodies, and it would be strange if dancing were not one of the city's favourite pastimes. The Viennese do indeed love to dance, but unlike some other large cities where there is dancing all the year round, here it is more or less concentrated on the *Fasching*, carnival time. Of course there are bars and night clubs for dancing, but except for one or two restaurants there are no dinner dances—the very idea makes the food-loving Viennese squirm—and no 'Palais de Danse'.

Once Christmas is past there is dancing everywhere. Each day a list of the balls taking place appears in the press. There are the fashionable Philharmoniker Ball, held in the buildings of the Gesellschaft der Musikfreunde, the Jägerball, which each year draws the upper crust dressed in dirndl and national costume to the Sophiensäle, whether they are interested in hunting and shooting or not, or something like the 'Ball of the Sons and Daughters of the Butchers in the Twelfth District' held in the local *Gasthaus*. This is the time when young girls of seventeen or eighteen and their partners are feverishly practising the waltz, both to the right and left, because to be one of the opening dancers at one of the society balls is any girl's dream and means that she has come out. Lines of young girls all in white, with their black-garbed, white-tied partners, wait for the first beat of Ziehrer's *Fächerpolonaise*, with which balls usually begin. After the official opening, with speeches which seem endless, comes the first waltz, with a swirl of white tulle and taffeta and silk, amid banks of flowers and glittering chandeliers. The most perfect setting for this is the Opera House, which for one night of the year, the night of the Opera Ball, turns into a fairy palace. The stalls are covered, so that the stage seems to spread across the huge oval of the entire theatre; the boxes and galleries are decorated with thousands of white and scarlet carnations, the lucky girls chosen for the opening committee wear tiny crowns, and among all this splendour lovely women and distinguished men from all over the world can be watched like marionettes on a stage. Anyone who has neither the obligatory white tie and tails nor sufficient funds for a ball ticket can get a ticket for the onlookers' gallery, and from the 'gods' can watch the whirling and swirling below far into the night.

The traditional ending to a ball is to take a taxi around 6 a.m. and go to some all-night pub to have a goulash and beer before either falling exhausted into bed or changing into workaday clothes for going to school or office. Or, if it happens to be Sunday, perhaps making a later start, and spending part of the day in the Vienna Woods.

Walking in the Vienna Woods on Sundays is a tradition that has been swept away by the motor-car. For us and for many others Sunday walks were almost as obligatory as Sunday Mass. They usually meant spending the whole day in the country, and in this way we became very familiar with all of Vienna's lovely surroundings. Nowadays large parts of the Vienna Woods remain unvisited even on the loveliest Sunday.

During the thirties Sunday walkers were for a time greatly
excited and distressed by the decision to build a broad, sweeping
motor road right through the Vienna Woods and up to Leopoldsberg and Kahlenberg. The main purpose was to alleviate unem-
ployment. Today the Höhenstrasse is one of the sights of Vienna,
and people do at least drive up into the woods and go for short
walks there even if they don't manage much more. Vienna seen
from the Kahlenberg or Cobenzl on a warm summer night is an
astonishingly beautiful sight. To the left the dark glittering waters
of the Danube flow serenely past, while to the right and beyond
the Danube are myriads of quivering lights. Up here there is
always life and company, but by walking just a little way off into
the beech forests—particularly if it is a weekday—it is easy to
forget that the city is so near and to become submerged in a
mellow country atmosphere of light and shade, the sweet scent
of wild strawberries and of lilies of the valley or the pungent one
of thyme and bergamot. It is only quite recently that the Vienna
Woods have been 'discovered'. A hundred and fifty years ago the
ascent of the Hermannskogel, the highest peak among the gentle
hills here, was acclaimed as a daring adventure. It was during the
Biedermeier epoch that nature came into its own and with it the
forests and meadows embracing Vienna on three sides. Often
when I have sat beneath the Breite Föhre, the spreading pine,
near Mödling, I have thought of the painting of that name by
Schnorr, which shows the selfsame tree and at its foot crino-
lined, corkscrew-curled ladies resting on the grass as happily as
we do today.

Any who want to get away from it all seek the depths of the
woods, while others who want to be in a crowd make for the
Prater at the other end of Vienna. From the Cobenzl it can be
seen quite easily. As always the spire of St Stephen's in the centre
of the city must be one's guide, and turning slightly to the left
of the church one can see the Giant Wheel and beyond it green
bunched trees right down to the Danube.

The Prater—from the Spanish word *Prado*, a meadow, for there is no getting away from historical associations and reminders of Hapsburg dominions—is a large riverside forest. Even today there are some magnificent trees left, and although it is no longer a game preserve—we must go farther afield, across the Danube into the Lobau for that—it is still a quiet, endless-seeming, park-like maze of meadows and shrubberies, romantic pathways twisting in and out between small ponds and former Danube promontories. Only a small section of it, the so-called Wurstel-prater, or Volksprater, offers the sort of popular entertainment which appeals to those looking for excitement.

In *The Third Man* the Giant Wheel, put up for the World Exhibition in 1873, turned almost menacingly above the fairgrounds, which shortly after the war consisted of little but rubble and bomb ruins. It was rather eerie in those days, with black marketeers and worse using it as a rendezvous. All that has changed, and even if the Prater is not exactly what it was before the war it is once again ablaze with lights, the air shattered with screaming wheels and raucous voices inviting you to step inside and see, possibly, the wonders of the East, a ventriloquist or conjurer, not to mention an increasing number of strip-teasers. On Saturday and Sunday afternoons it is the children and their parents who populate the Prater—there are still sufficient old-fashioned merry-go-rounds and scenic railways to capture any child's imagination. The evenings belong to the teenagers and grown-ups, bumping madly along in dodgem cars, displaying huge bunches of gaudy paper flowers or ludicrously ornate dolls won at one of the innumerable shooting booths. The *Gasthaus* gardens are filled to overflowing, though the famous Ladies' Orchestra which was one of the Prater's main attractions at the end of the last century has long ago been replaced by loudspeakers and canned music.

Beer is the favourite drink here, to go with frankfurters and large black radishes, thinly sliced and served with oil and vinegar. Barrow boys thrust them into your hands, and in the autumn months women with steaming kettles of water flourish golden cobs of corn to attract your attention to that rural delicacy which it is difficult to resist. As at the *Heuriger* there is a feeling of anonymity here, but while at the former there is relaxation and joviality, mixed with an air of romantic melancholy, in the Prater nerves are taut, there is excitement in the air, the underworld does not seem far away, so that amidst all the good-humoured nonsense we find ourselves looking for the streak of bitterness which is part of this world of make-believe.

But, as I say, the Wurstelprater is only a diminutive section of the Prater. Here too are trotting and flat-racing tracks, the Stadium, the biggest football ground in Vienna and the Messegelände, the trade fair ground, which continues to expand each year. We can play tennis here or golf, the bridle paths offer ideal riding country and horses can be hired at nearby stables. The *Lilliputbahn*, a miniature railway, puffs merrily along through the maze of trees and bushes, and at Whitsuntide the decorated Confirmation carriages used to roll along the seemingly endless, dead straight Hauptallee at a spanking pace.[1] This was the scene of the famous Flower Corso—famous not only for the splendour of the flowers displayed but also for the dressed-up crowd which came to watch it. One can imagine what a lovely sight it was beneath the white brilliance of chestnut after chestnut. The Hauptallee ends at the Lusthaus, the former hunting-lodge of the Emperor Joseph II, a charming octagonal building in the traditional yellow and green which now houses a restaurant.

Large though the Prater is, it is always alive with people, because the Viennese love it. As long ago as the early Middle Ages one of Vienna's traditional feasts took place here. In early spring the Court would take its pleasure in the riverside woodlands, and courtiers and their ladies would search for the first violet. The Duke himself was ready to receive it, honour its finder and declare that spring had arrived.

[1] Today, with a new local law forbidding all 'four-wheel' traffic along it, pedestrians have come into their own.

Chapter 8

Three-star Sights, and Others

SIGHTSEEING can be hard work, rushing from place to place anxious not to miss anything, and ending by remembering very little of what has been seen. In Vienna there are plenty of chances of seeing the sights the leisurely way.

When the weather is fine look around the centre of the city and stroll through its many parks. Even while you relax on a bench you are still surrounded by 'sights'. The shady Burggarten used to be the Emperor's private garden. It nestles close to the Hofburg and from wherever you may be standing, its walls or the spire of the Augustinerkirche are visible. In the early spring the glass-houses are opened to the public and they are a fairyland of massed banks of rhododendron, lilac and azaleas in the tropical atmosphere which produces innumerable orchids, while outside there may still be snow and ice.

In the early summer it is the Volksgarten close to the Ballhaus-platz, the Austrian Foreign Office, that most attracts. Here there are open-air restaurants, some rural, others smart enough for an evening's dancing. The water-lilies on the formal pond before the white marble monument of Empress Elisabeth stir gently as brilliant goldfish dart by, and all around is the scent of roses, borne across from the rose garden. There are thousands of roses— and each year new varieties are added to this immeasurable wealth of bush roses and ramblers, old-fashioned, high-stemmed blooms and new cultivations to dazzle the eye and enchant the nose.

Across the way from the Burgtheater and lying to right and left of the Rathaus, the Town Hall, is the Rathaus Park. Here it is the fountains, their white brilliance gushing endlessly towards the sky, which catch the eye, while in the Stadtpark, the largest park in the centre of the city, laid out a hundred years ago, the attraction is the quiet lake with its shady trees. Families of wild ducks nest here; in the summer storks, pelicans and flocks of peacocks cross its paths, and during Easter week the children's delight are the white rabbits and curly lambs which suddenly appear. Monuments abound, the most famous and popular being that of Johann Strauss, condemned for ever to play his violin within a bower of pale marble waifs.

There are other retreats, but few strangers know about them. How many, I wonder, discover the Heiligenkreuzerhof? To the left of the Universitätskirche—the Jesuit church—runs a narrow passageway known as Jesuitengasse. The church itself seems beautifully poised on its small square, its imposing façade and twin spires characteristic of early baroque architecture, but not typically Viennese. The interior, for Viennese taste too Italianate, is filled with elaborately carved, twisted pillars and a painted ceiling full of movement and including an illusory dome which makes one marvel at the artist's skill. The Jesuitengasse leads into the Schönlaterngasse, one of the oldest streets in Vienna, with houses from the fifteenth and sixteenth centuries. A red shimmer of flames and the sound of metal struck upon metal come from an old smithy where delicate wrought-iron work as well as heavy locks and bolts are still being made. A little farther to the left the odd figure of a cock-cum-dragon upon the façade of No. 7 makes us look up. The house, the Basilisken Haus, is closely linked with strange legends about a well that stood in its courtyard and in which a baker's apprentice once saw the terrible basilisk, that mythical reptile hatched by a serpent from a cock's egg. The stench of its sulphurous breath filled the neighbourhood, and it was only after various attempts at its destruction had failed that it was ensnared with a trick. A mirror was let down the well, and the monster's bloodshot, fatal eye proved its own undoing.

A few steps farther along is a narrow postern gate which a stranger may overlook, particularly since the Schönlaterngasse makes a sharp turn to the left to emerge in the Sonnenfelsgasse.

Every time I go through this gate, although I know so well what lies beyond it, I am filled anew with delight. The courtyard into which the gate opens is large even by modern standards, not merely compared with the cramped streets surrounding it. Enclosed on four sides by solid, plain buildings it is partly paved with large stone slabs and partly covered with gravel, so that there is something rustic about it, and the two delicate baroque pillars, topped with stone vases and joined together with a playful arabesque to form a gateway, come as a surprise. Beyond this there are mulberry trees, and the adjoining modest building is graced with a small onion spire and boasts two entrances, one plain and pedestrian, the other ornate and baroque.

This is the Heiligenkreuzerhof. Formerly most of the large Benedictine and Cistercian monasteries which had their seats in Lower or Upper Austria also kept establishments in Vienna, but this is the only one which remains as it has always been. It still belongs to the Cistercians of Heiligenkreuz Abbey. Its wine cellars are here, and the simple doorway which leads into the busy wine shop must not be confused with its more decorative neighbour, the entrance to the St Bernhard's Kapelle, a perfect little jewel of a baroque chapel. A few old-fashioned craftsmen have their diminutive shops in other wings of the building, which is now divided into flats, but there never seems to be any movement in the courtyard, and as you walk slowly across its full length of some three hundred yards to the second postern gate, which leads into the Grashofgasse and back to modern life, you draw deep breaths of countrified air to replenish petrol-laden lungs.

The Schottenhof is by comparison very much more lively and businesslike. It is attached to the Benedictine Schottenstift itself and you come through the classical entrance to meet that odd, slightly acid scent of wine and beer mingling with pungent paprika fumes from goulash casseroles simmering for ever in the depth of a *Gasthaus* kitchen. The centre of the courtyard is divided into two adjoining gardens, both sheltered by chestnut trees from which strings of fairy lights twinkle at night. The one

F

belongs to the wine shop of the Abbey, to which a *Gasthaus*, the Schottenkeller, is attached, the other to a coffee-house. The green rustic benches of the one and the white, twisted iron chairs of the other are patronized equally on long summer days. This juxta-position of wine and coffee is very characteristic of Viennese life.

Not far away from the Schottenhof another pungent scent—which, alas, has lost much of its familiarity—may stop you in your tracks. Here in the Augustinerstrasse you may just be in time to see the police hold the traffic back as, each day shortly before ten o'clock, the graceful and measured procession of white horses emerges from the lovely Renaissance courtyard beyond which they are stabled to cross the street and disappear into the Winter Riding School on the other side.

If you follow them you will see a note stating that every week-day between 10 and 12 a.m., the horses of the Spanish Riding School may be watched at work. Instead of merely watching their impeccable and superb performance on a Sunday it is worth paying the few schillings to go and see how this perfection comes about.

There is of course a sense of perfection even about the Winter Riding School itself—a pure white oblong, the only touch of colour being the yellow sand in the arena and the painting of the Emperor Charles VI in the royal box. It is the work of the younger Fischer von Erlach and was finished about 1735. On week-days visitors do not have fixed places but wander about, often to dis-cover that all the seats in the lower gallery have been taken, and so to climb up the narrow winding staircase to the upper gallery from which there is just as good a view of the prancing, superbly controlled horses.

There may be only about eight horses in the arena, so one can watch them closely. Soon one recognizes those who are already masters of their difficult craft, who set their feet with such pre-cision, whose every movement is a graceful synthesis of muscle play and rhythm. Others at the beginning of their training are fiery or frolicsome, but patiently and relentlessly their trainers lead them through the elementary paces until they become second nature to them.

The history of these unique white horses goes back to 1580, when the Archduke Charles, son of the Emperor Ferdinand I, bought a stud farm in Lipizza, not far from Trieste. For three hundred years the healthy, briny sea winds provided the atmosphere for the breeding ground of these animals. The finest stallions were always taken away to Vienna for breaking in and training in the Winter Riding School, and in time they returned to their original home to father equally fine sons and daughters. The race itself remained thoroughbred, and it is only during the past century that some Arab blood has been added—easily recognizable when one compares the rather heavy, ramses noses of the pure Lipizza stock with the concave, flaring nostrils of the Arabs. When after the First World War Trieste fell to Italy the stud farm was moved to Piber in Styria. It returned to Piber after its adventures at the end of the Second World War—the American General Patton saved the horses from deportation to the Russian zone by promptly having them removed into his own zone. Here in the paddocks and stables the sight of brilliantly white mares nuzzling coal-black foals must have surprised many visitors who do not know that the horses' final colour emerges only when they are fully grown. The Lipizza horses are late starters, for they are not ready for training until they are eight years old, and they reach the height of their capacity at about fourteen years.

Nowhere except in Vienna can the *Hohe Schule*, the art of horsemanship as practised by the nobility in the seventeenth century, still be found. In those days the various paces were practised not merely for the sake of their beauty but also because of their usefulness in battle. Watching the *Lipizzaner* perform is very much akin to watching Russian ballet.

The expressions used in training have remained unchanged through the centuries. There is the *Passage*, the first, essential movement to be learnt, in which the horse takes small steps but always on the same spot. The *Pillarde* are the two pillars in the centre of the hall to which the horses are hitched during their first lessons; the *Levade* means the horse sitting back on its haunches as if to beg. This is followed by many more exacting figures until the most difficult of all, the *Capriole*, is reached; for this the horse must leap into the air with all four feet simultaneously and, in mid air, lunge out as if to kick. The names of the horses, too, are majestic and old. Each one bears the name of its father and mother, and the five male lines which continue to repeat themselves appear on many of the shields above the horse boxes, the most famous perhaps being 'Maestoso' and 'Favory'.

It is difficult to drag oneself away from these horses and their quiet, brown-coated riders with their characteristic black cocked hats. It is not difficult to imagine the many-pillared, elegant hall as it was in the days of the Vienna Congress, when it was used not as a riding school but as a ballroom, for *redoutes* and fancy dress balls. Various paintings and engravings give a clear picture of these stupendous revels, and it is a puzzle how anyone was able to move around, let alone dance, in those lavishly dressed crowds.

The Winter Riding School is part of the Hofburg, and so is that other 'major sight', the Schatzkammer. This is the collection of crown jewels, historic emblems and ecclesiastic masterpieces which has been assembled in Vienna in the course of its history. An English friend I took to see the collection stood fascinated in front of the regalia of the Holy Roman Empire.

'It isn't the real thing, is it? It can't be, it must be a copy.' But of course it is not a copy.

The crown of the Holy Roman Empire itself was probably fashioned in A.D. 962 for the coronation of the Emperor Otto I. Massive and almost like a helmet, the huge jewels closely set within a network of gold, the central panel topped by a cross from which a bow leads to the back, it lies in a glass case beside the orb and sword and surrounded by an aura that is almost mystical.

For 800 years the emperors of the Holy Roman Empire were

crowned with it and the Hapsburg dynasty itself was crowned with it for many centuries. The last of them was the Emperor Franz II, last of the Holy Roman Emperors. After Napoleon had had himself crowned Emperor of France and the Holy Roman Empire itself slowly disintegrated he proclaimed himself Emperor of Austria, and replaced the ancient crown with the newer Austrian imperial crown, a beautiful Renaissance piece of work which had formerly been used as the royal crown of Hungary and Bohemia.

There are other crowns in the Treasury, among them the crown Napoleon had made for himself as King of Italy, and a diamond crown which belonged to the Empress Elisabeth. Maria Theresa's jewels are here, included in the Treasury long before her death because, having lost her husband, Charles of Lorraine, she insisted that as a widow she no longer wished to bedeck herself with finery. Here too are the insignia of the Golden Fleece, that greatest of all orders of chivalry, and the silver cradle of Napoleon's son, the King of Rome, its cool, empire lines and classic *décor* in striking contrast to so much splendour.

A royal death was often accompanied with even more pomp and circumstance than a royal birth. Traditionally the bodies of members of the House of Hapsburg were buried in the crypt below the Capuchin Church on the Neue Markt.

Nowadays the Kaisergruft beneath the Capuchin Church, where 136 members of the Hapsburg family are buried, is little more than a first-class tourist attraction. How this would have shocked Empress Anna, who in 1617 bequeathed the present-day church to the Capuchin friars on condition that a burial place for herself and her husband, the Emperor Matthias, was found there. The small rooms which constituted the original crypt were soon filled, so that the Emperor Ferdinand III's sarcophagus had to be placed across those of the Emperor Matthias and the Empress Anna until the crypt was enlarged. It now consists of eight rooms, and only members of the imperial family are buried here, with the one exception of the Gräfin Fuchs, Maria Theresa's governess, whom she wished to honour in this way. Maria Theresa not only added a considerable extension to the crypt, but the double sarcophagus which she had built for herself and her husband is perhaps the show-piece of the whole place.

After the exuberance and the larger-than-life magnificence of the baroque sarcophagi of Leopold I, Charles VI and Maria Theresa comes the sudden austere simplicity of those of Joseph II and other members of the imperial family who died during his reign. But Duke Albert of Teschen, the husband of Maria Theresa's favourite daughter, Marie Christine, found a way round the ruling about unadorned copper coffins by having Canova build a magnificent white marble monument for his wife in the Augustinerkirche.

What must have been the feelings of Francis Joseph as he followed the sombre coffin of his only son, the Archduke Rudolf, who had died in Mayerling under such strange and tragic circumstances? The hunting-lodge at Mayerling was turned into a Carmelite Convent and in its peaceful and lovely surroundings in the Vienna Woods it is difficult to associate it with any sort of mystery. It is not far from Heiligenkreuz Abbey, one of the major 'sights' which the country round Vienna can offer, and the countryside is rich in places intimately associated with the city's history. The abbey is a Cistercian foundation going back to Babenberg days. The superb Romanesque church and the life of the monks have changed little in the course of centuries, and to walk into the silence of the cloisters, disturbed only by the water gushing from the fountain in the conduit, is like walking into another world. And yet the abbey is alive, its tradition unbroken, so that it seems easy to imagine the white- and black-garbed monks of long ago working, praying and sleeping here as do their successors.

Klosterneuburg Abbey, the other major monastic foundation of the Middle Ages, lies farther upriver and looks across to the Bisamberg, the final foothill of the Alps, as well as to the seemingly endless unbroken plains. Here Napoleonic and imperial troops faced each other on more than one occasion. There is still an old arm of the Danube here, the Alte Donau, which remained at the end of the last century when the mighty river was regulated and forced into a concrete bed. Today it is a Mecca of water sports, including not only sailing and rowing but Europe's most modern outdoor swimming pool, the Gänsehäufl. Farther afield there is the Lobau, vast riverside forests where deer and other wild life are a delight and where in springtime the eye can feast on meadows thickly carpeted with snowdrops, while pussy willows gently touch your cheeks as you pass by.

Sometimes, of course, it rains. Sometimes nothing seems to appeal to us, and in any case our feet are worn out. That is the moment to go to the Dorotheum.

As long ago as 1702 the Emperor Joseph II granted a patent to what was then known as the 'Imperial and Royal Inquiry and Pawnbroking Office'. As time went on the Inquiry Office became separated from the Pawnbroking Office and when the latter finally settled on the site of the former Dorothea Convent it soon became known as the 'Dorotheum' or, even more familiarly and affectionately, as 'die Tante Dorothee'.

You can still go there to pop your gold watch, or your best suit or your wireless set if you are in sudden need of ready cash, but the Dorotheum has also become the greatest auctioneering establishment in Austria—there are branches not only in different parts of Vienna but also in the provinces. Every afternoon, punctually at two, auctions take place in a variety of rooms, some of them palatial, others dreary and reminiscent of dusty schoolrooms. You can watch diamonds being knocked down for thousands of schillings, while next door hand-made lace doilies or horrors in the guise of glazed porcelain figures are being snapped up for a mere bob. Unless you really want to buy something, it is better to come without any money. After having sat there for a time it is almost impossible to resist temptation, and suddenly one has raised a hand and is landed with twelve engraved wineglasses (one slightly chipped), a copper tea kettle or possibly even a tea wagon with huge spidery wheels and delicate canework body. There is very little on earth which at one time or another does not find its way to the Dorotheum, and going there may become a disease difficult to cure.

Twice a year there are huge auctions of works of art of all kinds, at which dealers and connoisseurs gather from all over Europe. But even at these the poor ignoramus may strike lucky. A friend of mine once bought one rather ramshackle lot consisting of various prints, and one tattered oil painting which has now turned out to be almost certainly a Goya; while an impoverished antique dealer from the provinces, who year after year regularly and carefully went through everything that came up for auction, bid for and obtained for a few schillings a folder, damp and musty and covered with spots of mould, which beneath worthless prints and engravings contained sixteen drawings by the Austrian master Gustav Klimt. He had made this discovery on a viewing day some time before the auction and his agony at the thought that someone else might make a similar discovery is understandable.

Though the Dorotheum is an old-fashioned institution, it plays its part very aptly in a modern world, like so much else in Vienna that has adapted itself to the times. But it would be unfair to Vienna and the Viennese if the emphasis on history were to obscure its most successful modern aspects and the achievements of some of the memorable personalities who made them.

The Viennese love to boast: not blatantly, but almost deprecatingly they assure you of their worth, their prowess, their eminence in every field of learning. Every Viennese is the born tourist guide, and if you ask him the way you are likely to be swept through the whole town to be shown those particular sights no one but he knows about. He can enumerate too, a little vaguely perhaps but with the greatest zest and self-confidence, all the Nobel Prizes that his countrymen have won, all the inventions that were fathered in Vienna and all the medical wonders which first saw the light of day in his city.

Unfortunately most of what he says is likely to be true. I say

'unfortunately' because many of Vienna's great sons were bur-
dened with that mixture of self-confidence and diffidence that has
caused them to do great things only to let others profit from them.
Very few people outside Vienna know, for instance, that the first
petrol-driven car was invented by the Austrian Siegfried Marcus
—it stands, terrifyingly massive and elementary, in the technical
museum. The same goes for the first sewing-machine by
Madersperger, the first typewriter by Mitterhofer and—the first
supersonic rocket. Only a few years ago an old Viennese scientist,
Silvio Pirquet, who still wanders amiably through its streets, was
internationally honoured for having worked out, decades ago,
the exact formula for sending a rocket into orbit—the same
formula that is in use today.

The greatest Viennese scientific tradition is its medical one.
The world-famous geneticist Mendel did not work in Vienna but
it was a professor at the Agricultural University who 'redis-
covered' him. The Vienna School of Medicine at the turn of
the century was famous, and Viennese surgeons and clinicians
were sought after and quoted the world over. Many of them are
forgotten by the layman, but there was one medical man among
them who changed not only the world's ideas but also its vocabu-
lary—Sigmund Freud. Vienna seems to have been the right
breeding ground for his startling theories, both positive and
negative, and though much of his emphasis on sex must now
seem exaggerated, a great deal of modern psychiatry is still,
ultimately, based on his findings.

Medicine and music are closely linked in Vienna, where doctors
are not only some of the keenest concert-goers but are themselves
musicians—it would be instructive to make a census of all the
'medical' string quartets in Vienna. Medicine and the social
sciences are naturally closely related, and social security and health
insurance have been an accepted public service in Austria since
1888. As in some other countries the services, faced with mounting costs and mounting public demands, have found themselves
in deep financial waters, in which they seem likely to flounder for

some years yet. The Viennese Municipality, for many years
firmly in the hands of the Socialists, endeavours all the time to
improve its services and extend them. One endearing provision,
which I don't think is practised in any other metropolis, is that each
mother at the birth of a baby receives a huge parcel of baby clothes,
toilet articles and nappies, and even a savings book with an opening deposit for the new citizen. An added personal note is that
blue or pink is used to differentiate between boy and girl.

Vienna, like most large cities, has its housing problems. The
city has never suffered from real slums, but living conditions for a
large part of the population have been anything but rosy since the
destruction left by the last war. The Viennese are flat-dwellers
rather than householders, preferring to spend as little as possible
on their housing—most rents by European standards are fan-
tastically low—so as to have more left over for eating, clothes
and entertainment. There are, however, many working couples
who, while possibly living in two small rooms in the city (no
bath and the lavatory most likely along the passage) have a
garden with a little week-end hut in the suburbs, and these
colonies are a splendid defence against the ever-increasing petrol
fumes and lust for speed. Here is to be found that neighbourliness
which is completely lacking in the town, where one can live all
one's life in a particular block of flats without knowing anything
about those who live next door. The overriding personality in
any house is most often the *Hausmeister*, the *concierge*, whose sway
is still impressive, though the days are long past when only he
was able to let you into your block of flats after closing hours at
9 p.m.

The *Hausmeister* are great talkers and great grumblers, whether
because of the dirt that always seems to accumulate on the stairs
despite their labours or because 'they' have been up to something
again. 'They', here as elsewhere, are the powers that be both local
and national, and politics, as far as the population is concerned,
consists mostly of grumbles. This is particularly true of local
affairs, and while proudly telling the stranger what a wonderful

city Vienna is the citizens are vociferous amongst themselves about local scandals and local failings. Every tree that is felled to make way for a new building is a major tragedy up to the moment of its disappearance—after which it is completely forgotten. Every modern building is an utter horror, until, like the enormous Stadthalle, a combination of sports arena, concert hall and conference centre, which is indeed startlingly modern, it becomes fully accepted. Traffic innovations are fought against tooth and nail, are pooh-poohed and derided and are finally given nicknames, such as Jonas Grotte and Jonas Reindl for the two first major subway crossings at the Opera and Schottentor; Jonas being the name of the reigning mayor at the time of their construction and 'grotto' and 'casserole' being easily associated with these public utilities. These are now both sights proudly to be displayed to country cousins who try their first steps on fast-moving escalators.

Something no one grumbled about is an idea which is quickly spreading across Europe, but then it is based on private initiative and not official organization. This is the *Kinderdorf*, which the Tyrolean Hermann Gmeiner started to put into practice some twelve years ago. Just outside Vienna, in Hinterbrühl, lies the newest of these Children's Villages, and it is worth while combining a walk in the Vienna Woods with a visit to it. The aim of this revolutionary social innovation is very simple and completely logical. Orphans and neglected children, instead of being put into an institution of some sort, become members of a 'family' living in its own house in one of these villages. Each family consists of nine children of different ages and is in charge of a 'mother'. The *Kinderdörfer* are usually built close to ordinary villages or towns, so that the children can attend local schools and altogether lead a normal home life. Even when they are grown up they can return to their village and their mother for holidays, and in this way they become part of a family for life. To walk into one of these simply furnished but homely, modern and clean houses and feel the pulse of everyday life is heart-warming.

The *Kinderdorf* in the Hinterbrühl, with its atmosphere of optimism and of looking to the future, is an antidote to any feeling that Vienna since the Second World War has become a dying city. It seemed to be finished at the end of the First World War, but during the early thirties there was an upward trend; the Austrian schilling suddenly became the 'dollar of the Alps', Viennese workers' flats were world famous. Then came the Nazis and the Second World War and most people thought that this really was the end. They were wrong. Today Vienna is once more a living city—even statistically. For many years the death rate exceeded the birth rate; now the figures are reversed. Young people have faith again in their home town. The parks are full of small children and young mothers pushing prams. Buildings which for decades had turned grimy, crumbling façades towards visitors have suddenly emerged with new surfaces and bright colours. Vienna has become rejuvenated and presents a young face in an old setting. It is once more a city at home to all the world.

Index